Responses to 101 Questions on Islam

John Renard

PAULIST PRESS
New York / Mahwah, N.J.

Cover designs for this series are
by James Brisson Design & Production, Williamsville, Vermont

Library of Congress Cataloging-in-Publication Data

Renard, John,   1944–
    Responses to 101 questions on Islam / John Renard.
        p.   cm.
    Summary: Answers questions about the religious traditions of Islam and Muslims, arranged in such categories as Beginnings and Sources, History and Development, Beliefs and Practices, Law and Ethics, Cultural and Intellectual Themes, Women and the Family, and more.
    Includes index.
    ISBN 0–8091–3803–4 (alk. paper)
    1. Islam—Essence, genius, nature. [1. Islam—Miscellanea. 2. Questions and answers.] I. Title. II. Title: Responses to one hundred and one questions on Islam. III. Title: Responses to one hundred and one questions on Islam.
BP163.R46   1998
297—dc21   98–4301
                                                                                     CIP
                                                                                      AC

Published by Paulist Press
997 Macarthur Boulevard
Mahwah, New Jersey 07430

Printed and bound in the
United States of America

CONTENTS

For brothers and sisters—
mine and Mary Pat's—
Dick, Joe, Suzanne,
Tom, Brian, Rita, Sue,
and their spouses—
Kay, Tom, Paddy, Al and Greg

PREFACE

In 1992 Paulist Press published my introduction to Islamic spirituality and religious life entitled *In the Footsteps of Muhammad: Understanding the Islamic Experience*. Focusing on the central position of the prophet Muhammad, it took as its organizing principle the notion that a rich and complex interpretation of three journeys in Muhammad's life has shaped Islamic spirituality. The book described how Muslims have understood the three paradigmatic journeys—the Hijra (Emigration) from Mecca to Medina in 622 C.E., the Hajj or pilgrimage to Mecca, and the Isra/Mi'raj (Night Journey/Ascension)—not only historically but metaphorically as well. These are not only events that occurred during Muhammad's life, but ongoing models for subsequent generations of Muslims. Each of the three journeys functioned as a structural device within which to describe a number of related aspects of Islamic spirituality.

Because that earlier volume was slanted toward spirituality, it did not include much in the way of either historical developments or contemporary themes. The present volume is also very much an introduction to Islam, but its purpose is different. It revisits many of the main themes covered in *In the Footsteps of Muhammad*, but uses a different structure to that end and expands its coverage to include material beyond the scope of a study in spirituality. Still relatively brief, the present treatment naturally offers limited coverage of the vast subject of the Islamic religious tradition. But moving beyond the central themes of spirituality, it touches on philosophy and theology; matters of religious interest in Islamic history; questions concerning the relationships between religion and culture; themes in Islam's relationship to Judaism and Christianity; matters relating to women and family life; legal and

ethical problems; and a host of issues concerning Islam as a global phe-
nomenon in the twentieth century.

For over twenty-five years I have been talking about the religious
tradition called Islam in the contexts of secondary, university, and adult
education, largely in connection with Roman Catholic institutions and
less formal gatherings. Students and listeners have naturally had countless questions about this vast subject, but some queries have been peren-
nial favorites. These pages present a sample of the questions most asked
within the nine general topic categories in which I have arranged them.
A short bibliography suggests further reading that will offer greater
depth on the subjects introduced here. In addition, an appendix provides
a questionnaire to assist readers in assessing the state of their current
attitudes toward, and of the accuracy of present information about,
Islam. Readers may wish to take the questionnaire before reading, and
then again afterward, as an informal gauge.

Special thanks go to David Vila of Saint Louis University for the
superb editorial assistance that sped the project along. Thanks also to
the Hotfelder Distinguished Professorship in the Humanities, within the
College of Arts and Sciences of Saint Louis University, for the time and
resources it has afforded. I am grateful to Kevin Lynch of Paulist Press
for inviting me to write for this series. And thanks to my wife, Mary Pat,
for her unstinting companionship and support.

Companion volumes on Hinduism and Buddhism, using the same
nine-part structure as this volume for ready comparability, are now in
preparation for the "101 Questions" series.

John Renard
Saint Louis University

ONE:

BEGINNINGS AND SOURCES

THE 101 QUESTIONS AND RESPONSES

1. When and where did Islam come into being?

At almost fourteen hundred years old, Islam is one of the world's younger major religious traditions. It began in the early seventh century near the western edge of the Arabian peninsula in Mecca, an important city along the caravan route from Syria in the north to the Yemenite kingdoms of southwestern Arabia. Although Christians and Jews had long before taken up residence in various parts of Arabia, the prevailing religious climate was a kind of animism sometimes called *polydaemonism,* the worship of "many spiritual beings" thought to inhabit natural phenomena. Features of landscape, such as stones and springs, could take on a numinous aura and gradually become the focus of a sacred place. Some sites developed as the centers of cultic worship and pilgrimage, with one of the several local deities *(ilahat)* rising to prominence as the chief among them *(al-ilah,* "the" god).

By the late sixth century, Mecca had achieved the status of the principal cultic center, attracting large numbers of traders and pilgrims to its regular religious and cultural festivities. At the heart of the city was—and still is—the Ka'ba, which in Muhammad's time was a simple, nearly cubic-shaped structure of dark stone. In one of its four corners was set a black stone somewhat larger than a bowling ball, now fractured into seven pieces and framed in a collar of silver. Such stones had long been part of local religious centers, not only in the Arabian peninsula, but throughout the greater Middle East. In the Hebrew scriptures, stone pillars had been not only signs of contention, when they were at the center of idolatrous cults, but also acceptable symbols of help and witness. When Joshua, for example, gathered the people of

Israel together to renew their special relationship with God, he set up a stone and called upon it to witness in its mute integrity that the people had reaffirmed the covenant (Joshua 24). Popular Muslim tradition has it that the Ka'ba's black stone has likewise been taking note of momentous events—the rise and fall of the powerful and the making and breaking of oaths—since the very dawn of creation. At the appropriate moment, it will reveal all.

In Muhammad's time the Meccan cult revolved around a principal deity called Allah ("the" god, or simply God), whose three "daughters" (Allat, Manat, and Uzza) also figured in local piety. The Quraysh tribe had become the ruling authority over the city's affairs and exercised considerable control over the Ka'ba.

The Ka'ba and its stone had many meanings to the Meccans of Muhammad's day, and these would play an important role, sometimes negative and sometimes more positive, in the Prophet's life. According to one account, when the structure had to be rebuilt, the Meccans asked Muhammad the Trustworthy to replace the stone in its socket. Ever aware of the symbolic value of his public actions, and looking for ways to unify local factions, Muhammad placed the stone in the center of his cloak and had representatives of the chief interests lift it with him by grabbing a corner of the cloak. As the Quraysh came more and more to disapprove of Muhammad's new preaching, they applied the ultimate social pressure, denying him access to the sacred precincts to pray. Eventually the Ka'ba would become the center of the world of Islam. In the classic Islamic interpretation of history, the birth of Islam marked the death of the "age of ignorance" *(jahiliya)*.

2. What were some of the most important things happening in the Middle East and the greater Mediterranean world when Islam began?

Soon after the Roman Empire divided into West and East in the fourth century, Byzantium began to consolidate its power in the Eastern Mediterranean, taking control of much of the central Middle East and North Africa. By the time Rome fell in 476, the Byzantine Empire was well established in its own right. Along its southeastern fringe, in a line that ran from southern Egypt up through Syria and Iraq and across the

Caucasus almost to the Caspian Sea, the Byzantines had developed a "buffer state" in the Christian Arab tribe called the Ghassanids. Meanwhile, the Sasanian Persian Empire that ruled from eastern Iraq toward the east across what is now Iran, also had its own buffer state in the Arab tribe called the Lakhmids. Through their Arab surrogates these two powerful "confessional empires" (Christian and Zoroastrian) struggled back and forth across the region to the north of the Arabian peninsula, an area covering much of present-day Syria and Iraq.

The Sasanian Persian empire had supplanted the last major Roman Middle Eastern successor state, the Parthians, in the early third century. Before the end of that century the Sasanians had reestablished Zoroastrianism as the creed of the realm. Just around the time of Muhammad's birth, both of the confessional empires reached the zenith of their powers, Byzantium under the Emperor Justinian (527–565) and Sasanian Persia under Nushirvan (531–579). And as the Muslim community was beginning to grow in size and strength, the Byzantine and Sasanian states were embroiled in a protracted war (603–628) that would virtually exhaust the capability of both empires to project their control over the central Middle East. The resulting political vacuum set the stage for the emergence of the Muslim forces as a dominant power in the region.

3. Who was Muhammad? What do we know about his life in general?

Muhammad was born in Mecca around 570 C.E. to a rather poor family of the clan of Hashim, one of the branches of the Quraysh tribe. His father died before Muhammad was born and the boy's mother died when he was six years old. According to Arabian custom, the youngster was sent to be reared among the Bedouin. After his mother's death, Muhammad grew up in the custody first of grandfather Abd al-Muttalib and later in the house of his uncle Abu Talib, whose son Ali would later become a major religious and political figure as well. Tradition has it that the young Muhammad traveled with his uncle on business. One story relates that in Syria they met an old Christian monk named Bahira, who discerned the marks of prophetic greatness in the boy.

When Muhammad was about twenty-five, he married a widow fifteen years his senior. Khadija ran her own caravan business, and

Muhammad went to work for her. Muhammad would occasionally retreat to a nearby mountain to meditate and seek within the source of life. Around 610 C.E., when he had reached the age long considered in the Middle East a necessary precondition for the imparting of wisdom and ministry, Muhammad began to experience troubling visitations that sent him in turmoil to ask Khadija's counsel.

On the "Night of Power" now commemorated on the 27th of Ramadan, the earliest message commanded him to "Recite!" (literally, "make qur'an, recitation"), which no human being could know unaided. The encounter left him confused and uncertain. Not until as much as a year later did Muhammad hear a follow-up message of confirmation: "Indeed your Lord is the one who best knows who has strayed from His path, who best knows those who are guided" (Qur'an 68:7). Assured that he was not losing his sanity, Muhammad was attentive to the messages from the unseen world. From then on, revelations came more frequently. During the next several years, Muhammad slowly gathered a circle of "converts" who would form the nucleus of a faith community. Leaders of the Quraysh grew increasingly unhappy at the negative effects Muhammad's preaching was having on caravan and pilgrim traffic to the Ka'ba, as well as at the prospect of a rival leader in their midst. Around 615 C.E., under growing pressure and amid threats to the safety of his community, Muhammad sent a group off to seek asylum across the Red Sea with the Christian ruler of Abyssinia (Ethiopia). Muhammad remained in Mecca.

Under pressure from the leading Meccans, Muhammad had been investigating the possibility of moving his community from the increasingly hostile environment of Mecca to a safer haven. Hopeful prospects arrived in 621 C.E. with a delegation from Yathrib, a city several hundred miles north of Mecca. Looking for someone to help them negotiate a peaceful settlement to factional problems in their city, the representatives invited Muhammad to come and apply his already renowned talent for arbitration. Arrangements were finalized, and in 622 C.E. the Muslims headed north to Yathrib, whose name would soon change to Madinat an-Nabi ("City of the Prophet"), or simply Medina. That important journey was called the Hijra or Emigration, and marks the birthday of Islam, so to speak, and the beginning of the Muslim calendar (with dates marked A.H., "after the Hijra").

Muhammad's years in Medina, reflected in the text of the Qur'an as well as in later historical writing, witnessed major changes in his style of leadership and in the shape of the community of believers. Muhammad's prominence in the new setting gave prestige to the community. As the group increased, so did the demands on Muhammad's administrative time and skill, so that what began as spiritual leadership gradually grew into a more comprehensive oversight. During the "Medinan period," the Muslims also took up arms against the Quraysh and fought a number of battles with the Meccans. After nearly eight years of bitter conflict, the two sides struck a truce, and the Muslims were allowed to return to Mecca without opposition. In 630, Muhammad led a triumphal band to claim the city for the Muslims. Two years later, Muhammad returned to Mecca for what would be his farewell pilgrimage to the Ka'ba. He died in 632 after an illness of several months.

4. Do Muslims worship Muhammad? Do they attribute any special powers to him? What is his spiritual status?

Muslims have never considered Muhammad as any more than a very special human being, particularly favored by God. They universally revere him, hold him in the greatest esteem, and feel enormous depth of affection for him. Muhammad provides, first and foremost, the ultimate model of what God wants every human being to strive for. Of course, Muhammad was what he was by God's grace and power; one can neither aspire to, let alone achieve, the status of prophet by one's own effort. Muslims are quick to point out that Muhammad himself considered the Qur'an his only "miracle," but tradition and popular lore over the centuries have attributed a number of extraordinary experiences to the Prophet.

Nevertheless, in order to understand Muhammad's lofty spiritual status, one needs to appreciate some of the experiences he is said to have gone through. Tradition reports that on the twenty-seventh night of the month of Rajab in the year 621 C.E., Muhammad underwent a twofold mystical experience. In the first part, God "carried his servant by night, from the Mosque of the Sanctuary to the Farther Mosque" (Qur'an 17:1). Later interpreters would equate the first site with the shrine of the Ka'ba in Mecca, and the second with the southern end of the temple area in Jerusalem, where now stands an early eighth-century structure called "the Farther Mosque" *(al-masjid al-aqsa)*. This "Night Journey" *(isra')* was already clearly a kind of otherworldly experience, for ancient narratives place Muhammad in the company of earlier prophets in the Farther Mosque, and they naturally ask him to lead them in the ritual prayer. The second phase of the journey, however, called the "Ascension" *(mi'raj),* finds the Prophet riding a winged human-faced steed named Buraq and led by Gabriel toward the very throne of God. Marvelously embellished tales have developed around this experience. Vivid descriptions of Muhammad's excursion follow him through the various levels of heaven, where he meets all of his major prophetic forebears, down to the dark circles of hell where Gabriel shows him the horrors of the damned. This is truly the picture of a heroic journey of initiation in the mysteries of the unseen world. Many Muslims believe the journey involved physical locomotion, but a strong tradition of nonliteralistic interpretation has always regarded it as a spiritual and inward experience. However one interprets these moments in Muhammad's life, the power of the link tradition has forged between the Prophet and Jerusalem remains as great as ever and continues to be part of the mix in current events in the Middle East.

5. If Muhammad was not the only prophet, who were some of the others, and how do they fit into the Islamic scheme of things?

Jewish and Christian readers will already have some familiarity with the notion of the prophet and prophetic mission. Since time immemorial, prophet-types have played a major role in the religious history of the Middle East. In the Hebrew scriptures, prophets receive a mandate to speak on God's behalf. Their mission often requires that they stand up to the high and mighty, posing the divine challenge of justice for the powerless of the earth. The problem of how to discern true prophets from charlatans has exercised religious minds for millennia as well. In addition to the full-fledged prophets, lesser characters have also played a part. These include sages, oracles, and soothsayers.

All of these religious types were familiar to many people in the Arabia of Muhammad's day. But as Muhammad would discover, the majority of the populace welcomed the advent of a prophet no more enthusiastically in the seventh century C.E. than they would have in the seventh century B.C.E. Islamic tradition numbers over two dozen figures sent to particular peoples, including David, Solomon, Noah, and Jonah as well as the Arabian figures Hud, Salih, and Shu'ayb. All of them are "prophets" (*nabi,* pl. *anbiya'*) commissioned to warn their people; some are in addition "messengers" *(rasul,* pl. *rusul)* to whom scriptures are revealed. All of the prophets and messengers experienced rejection at the hands of their people, and some were even killed.

Muhammad readily identified with several of the prophets in particular, especially with Abraham, the "Friend of the Merciful" *(Khalil ar-Rahman)* and Moses, "God's Conversant" *(Kalim Allah)*. In Islamic tradition, Abraham was neither Jew nor Christian, but a *hanif,* a seeker after the one true God. As the Qur'an says: "Truly Abraham was a model (lit. an *umma*), obedient to God, and a seeker (lit. *hanif*) who assigned no partner to God. He responded in gratitude to the bounty of the one who chose him and guided him to the Straight Path....So We have revealed to you (Muhammad) that you should follow the believing ways (lit. *milla*) of Abraham the seeker...." (Qur'an 16:120–21, 123). It was Abraham who had prayed that God would "send among them a messenger from their midst who will unfold to them your signs and teach them the Book and the wisdom" (Qur'an 2:129).

Moses' importance in the Qur'an is equal to that of Abraham. "We sent Moses with Our signs: 'Bring your people out from profound darkness into the light and make them mindful of the days of God.' Truly in that are signs for all who are long-suffering and grateful" (Qur'an 4:5). Qur'an 73:15 likens Muhammad especially to Moses. Islamic tradition likewise sees a reference to Muhammad in the words of Deuteronomy 18:18, in which God says to Moses, "I will raise up for them a prophet like you from among their kinsmen, and will put my words in his mouth; he shall tell them all that I command him." Curiously, one text of the Qur'an (7:155–57) has God speaking approvingly to Moses of "those who follow the Apostle, the unlettered Prophet (i.e., Muhammad) whom they find written of (in their own) Torah and Gospel...." The allusion is apparently first to the text of Deuteronomy just mentioned, and secondly to references to the Paraclete in John 14–16.

Medieval Muslim theologians interpreted the Johannine text in a fascinating way. Speakers of Semitic languages such as Arabic become accustomed to find basic meanings in consonantal roots of words that, when written, are without their vowels. Transferring that way of thinking to Greek, scholars reasoned that Christians had misread Jesus' term as *parakletos,* "Advocate or counselor," interpreted by Christians as the Holy Spirit. A simple insertion of the correct vowels would yield *periklutos,* "the highly praised one," and thus a meaning more acceptable to Muslims. The name Muhammad in Arabic derives from the root *HaMaDa,* "to praise." When Arabic wants to intensify a root meaning, it doubles the middle consonant, hence *HaMMaDa,* "to praise highly." In order to express the idea that a particular individual has been praised highly, Arabic forms a passive participle by prefixing *mu-* and producing the word *muHaMMaD,* the "highly praised one."

What is most important to note in all this is the Muslim conviction that God sends a message to suit every circumstance perfectly. As the Qur'an says, "We (God) have sent no messenger except with the language of his people, that he might give them clarity. God allows to wander off whom He will, and He guides whom He will" (Qur'an 4:4).

6. How did the Muslim scripture, the Qur'an, develop and what sort of a book is it?

Written in Arabic, the Qur'an is roughly the size of the New Testament, and is divided into 114 chapters called "suras." Unlike either the Hebrew or Greek testaments, however, the Qur'an unfolded over a relatively short period of time, and its articulation is attributed to only one human being. Beginning in about 610 C.E., when he was about forty years old, Muhammad began to experience, in mostly auditory but occasionally visual form, what he would come to identify as divine revelations. Muhammad initially delivered the message orally, and it was not until more than two decades after the Prophet's death that a more or less definitive text was compiled and written. Tradition has divided the text into two main periods, the Meccan and Medinan, corresponding to the years before and after the Hijra, the move to Medina in 622 C.E. Scholars have more recently further divided the Meccan period into very early, early, middle, and late periods, on the basis of the form and content of the suras.

Five themes appear most often in the earliest suras. Evidently presuming belief in some deity on the part of their hearers, they emphasize

God's creative power, providence, and guidance. There was at first no emphasis on belief in only one God. Second, they speak of accountability at judgment in a rather general way, without specific reference to particular reward or punishment as motivation for upright behavior. In view of these two, the suras suggest that the appropriate response for the individual is a combination of gratitude and worship. The former flows out of an inner recognition of one's total dependence on God expressed formally in prayer. Parallel social consequences are acknowledged in the need for generosity as expressed in giving to those in need and in seeking a just distribution of wealth. Finally the early message includes the theme of Muhammad's dawning awareness of his own prophetic mission and all that it would demand of him.

During the middle Meccan period, both the tone and the content of the suras began to change. Stories first of indigenous Arabian and then of biblical prophets illustrated graphically the disastrous consequences attendant upon refusal to hear the prophetic message. Here one finds a growing insistence on monotheistic belief and forthright condemnation of idolatry. Toward the end of the Meccan period, emphasis on the rejection of past prophets grew apace with Muhammad's own experience of local opposition.

During the Medinan period, 622–632 C.E., both the style and the content changed dramatically. Whereas the Meccan suras tended to be poetic in tone, a form called rhymed prose *(saj')*, and quite dramatic, the later message became more proselike. Its content reflected the growing need to regulate the daily life of the expanding community of Muslims, and the reality of increased contact with Christians and Jews (of whom several large tribes played a major part in the life of Medina).

Over a period of twenty-three years or so, the divine interventions would come upon Muhammad in a variety of circumstances, often at times when he was struggling with a particular problem or issue. For example, for a while after the Hijra, the Muslims faced Jerusalem when they prayed, as did the local Jews. Apparently some friction caused a falling-out with the Jewish community, causing Muhammad concern over the continued symbolic statement of the prayer orientation. In response came the revelation, "We have seen you turning your face about toward the heavens. We shall now turn you toward a direction *(qibla)* that you will find satisfying. Turn your face toward the Mosque of the Sanctuary (site of the Ka'ba in Mecca); wherever you are, turn your faces toward it" (Qur'an 2:144). That verse sometimes serves as a decorative inscription over the *mihrab* (niche) in mosques, which indicates the direction of Mecca.

7. Do Muslims have any other religious books that they consider authoritative?

Second only to the Qur'an in sacred authority are the "sayings" of Muhammad, enshrined in a large body of literature called Hadith. The Hadith literature is similar to the Gospels to the extent that it preserves the words and deeds of the religious founder.

The record of Muhammad's words and deeds evolved gradually. For several generations at least, Muslims hesitated to put the words into writing, perhaps out of concern that the words of the Prophet be kept separate from the Word of God in the Qur'an. Some hadiths were written down, but memory of Muhammad's sayings and actions remained alive largely through oral transmission, recollections passed on from one generation to another. Curiously, the early Muslims sought to remember not only *what* Muhammad had said and done, but *who transmitted* the material as well. Some members of local communities came to be known as particularly important living repositories of the tradition. Several generations along, religious scholars were becoming increasingly concerned that the living link might eventually weaken to the breaking point. So toward the end of the eighth and the beginning of the ninth century, nearly two hundred years after Muhammad's death, traditionists mounted a vast concerted effort to gather all available evidence of the living record.

Their "search for Hadith" took the collectors across the central Islamic lands, interviewing countless individuals known for reliable powers of recollection. But collecting was not the end of the process. Scholars then subjected the material to intense scrutiny, inquiring into the background and trustworthiness of every individual named among the chains of transmitters *(isnad)* associated with each saying. Analysis of such personal characteristics as veracity, intellect, uprightness, and devotion, along with other data concerning the times and places individuals had lived, allowed scholars to classify transmitters as part of the emerging "science of men." A single weak link in a chain would indicate an unreliable hadith.

By the end of the ninth century, a group of six major collections had come to be regarded as authoritative among Sunni Muslims, each containing thousands of sayings with assessments of their reliability. There are dozens of others as well, and Shi'i Muslims also developed several major collections of their own. Like the Gospels, the Hadith are considered divinely revealed. But whereas Muslims consider the Qur'an the direct literal word of God, the Hadith represent content of divine origin couched in Muhammad's own unique expression.

8. What happened when Muhammad died? How did the Muslims carry on where he left off?

Muhammad's death thrust the young community into a protracted debate over the criteria of legitimate succession. According to sources compiled as much as two or three centuries after Muhammad's death in 632 C.E., two predominant solutions to the problem of succession emerged. One group maintained that the Prophet had explicitly designated his son-in-law Ali to be his Caliph (literally, "successor" or "vicegerent"). The other, convinced that Muhammad had made no such appointment, opted for the procedure of choosing from among a group of elder Companions of Muhammad. They chose Muhammad's father-in-law Abu Bakr. The group that supported Ali's candidacy came to be called the Shi'a ("party," "supporters") of Ali, popularly known as Shi'ites. Those who backed Abu Bakr were in the majority and formed the nucleus of what came to be called the "People of the Sunna and the Assembly," Sunnis for short. Ali's backers continued to insist that Ali was unfairly passed over three times, gaining only in 656 C.E. the leadership role that had been his by right for nearly thirty-five years.

The well-known distinction between Sunni and Shi'i identifies only the largest institutional division within the Muslim community. Muslims are quick to point out that none of these so-called "divisions" indicates any noteworthy variations in belief and practice among the world's one billion Muslims. Still, major classical sources from within the tradition have seen fit to describe their own history in terms of these allegiances.

9. Christians talk about an "apostolic age" that extended beyond the lifetime of Jesus. Do Muslims have anything similar, an idealized period that lives on as a time uniquely informed by the spirit of the founder?

Islamic tradition early on developed an intense interest in the importance of direct links to the Prophet. First-generation Muslims, who had enjoyed the great blessing of living in Muhammad's presence, came to be called the Companions *(sahaba)*. Their authority in matters of religious judgment ranks second only to that of the Prophet. In matters of dispute about how to interpret the Qur'an and sayings of Muhammad, the views of the Companions became the first recourse. Tradition further classifies Companions according to such criteria as their seniority in Islam, degree of participation in crucial events (such as the battles of Badr and Uhud), and whether they were among those who made the Hijra with Muhammad. As a group, the Companions have come to be revered much as Christians revere the Apostles of Jesus. Christians need only recall how eager Paul was to establish his rank among the Apostles, even though he had never met Jesus, to appreciate the importance of such a socioreligious classification.

Four of the most important Companions are those who, in the Sunni view, were Muhammad's earliest successors in leadership and became known as "the Rightly Guided Caliphs." Muhammad's father-in-law Abu Bakr (d. 634) was chosen first. His first task was to bring back to the Islamic fold a number of Bedouin tribes for whom Muhammad's death triggered a return to their ancestral ways. Already advanced in age, Abu Bakr was among the few early caliphs to die of natural causes. Umar ibn al-Khattab succeeded Abu Bakr and ruled for about ten years (d. 644). Umar was especially noted for his firm administrative style, and is perhaps most famous for wresting the city of Jerusalem from Byzantine control. (The Dome of the Rock is popularly but erroneously called "The Mosque of Umar.") After Umar was killed, a council appointed Uthman ibn Affan, a member of the Quraysh family, and he administered the growing Islamic sphere of influence until he was murdered in 656. During the twenty-four years following Muhammad's death, the caliphs administered from the city of Medina, but that would soon change.

Muhammad's cousin Ali ibn Abi Talib came to the fore. His supporters, the "Shi'a" or "faction" of Ali, now known collectively as Shi'i

Muslims, would argue that the first three caliphs had been usurpers. At last, they believed, the man who should have been the first caliph could assume his rightful place. Ali's stormy five-year tenure witnessed deepening fissures within the community and a heightened level of strife. Ali had built a base of support in the Iraqi garrison town of Kufa and so moved the capital there. Stiffest opposition came from Mu'awiya, the recently appointed governor of Damascus, who was a cousin of Uthman, the third caliph. Mu'awiya and his clan were convinced Ali had been complicit in the murder of Uthman and determined to avenge their kinsman's death. Ironically, it was a dissident who had originally been among Ali's Shi'a who would murder this fourth and last of the "Rightly Guided" caliphs, thus effectively ending the Islamic analog to Christianity's "apostolic age." The immediate descendants of the Companions came to be known as the Followers *(tabi'un),* and their views on substantive issues rank next in authority. Together with the previous and succeeding generations (called the "Followers of the Followers"), they comprise the category of the "predecessors" *(salaf).* As in most traditional views of religious history, Muslims regard the time of Muhammad himself as the pinnacle after which all else is spiritual entropy.

10. How did Islam develop and spread during the first decades after Muhammad's death?

Very soon after the Prophet's death, in 632, Muslim forces began to move out of the Arabian peninsula effectively for the first time. After Abu Bakr united most of the Arab tribes under the banner of Islam, Umar spent much of his ten-year rule conquering the regions that now constitute the heart of the central Middle East. To the north, his forces ended the Byzantine domination of the Fertile Crescent, including Iraq, greater Syria, and the holy city of Jerusalem. Further to the west, Umar established garrisons in Egypt. And to the east, he made serious inroads into the realm of the Zoroastrian Sasanian dynasty of Persia.

Umar was responsible for the initial establishment of the military and financial mechanisms that would form the basis of subsequent expansion. That included the practice of setting up garrison towns in the subjugated territories. Growing out of a policy designed to allow maximum self-determination of the subject populations, the use of garrison towns was meant to keep the conquering forces apart except when needed to maintain order. Two ancient garrisons that went on to become important Iraqi cities, for example, are Kufa and Basra. Conquered peoples were allowed to continue practicing their ancestral faiths; the Muslims did not follow a policy of forced conversion. There is considerable evidence that Christian communities fed up with oppressive Byzantine rule cooperated broadly with the invading Muslims.

During the twelve-year tenure of Uthman, Muslim forces made further decisive gains against the Byzantine empire to the north as far as the Caucasus. To the west, he expanded into what is now Libya and developed naval forces capable of challenging Byzantine control of the Mediterranean. He brought down the Sasanian empire and pushed the eastern border of Islamdom well into Persia. According to tradition, at Uthman's order an official "standardized" written version of the Qur'an was produced.

When Uthman was murdered in 656, the first of two disastrous civil wars that would mark the second half of the seventh century broke out. For the next five years or so, Ali fought a losing battle to establish his legitimacy as universal Muslim leader. His power base gradually eroded, while that of his chief rival, Mu'awiya, grew to such an extent that Mu'awiya had himself proclaimed caliph in Jerusalem in 660. The following year Ali was murdered by a disaffected former supporter, Ali's son Hasan capitulated to Mu'awiya, and the first of the great dynasties, the Umayyad, came to birth with its capital in Damascus.

TWO:

HISTORY AND DEVELOPMENT

11. Why did Islam spread so quickly? Was it a political rather than a "missionary" movement?

Rapid as Islam's spread was during the reigns of Muhammad's four immediate successors, the Rightly Guided Caliphs, it enjoyed still more dramatic expansion during the subsequent fifty years or so. Under the earliest caliphs of the Umayyad dynasty, Muslim armies had pushed westward across North Africa, rooting out the last vestiges of Byzantine power in Carthage, and had crossed the Straits of Gibraltar by 711. In Spain they encountered and defeated the Arian Visigoths of King Roderick. Within eight years they had established an administrative center in the city of Cordoba, and by 732 the Muslim armies had crossed the Pyrenees into France. There Charles Martel halted their advance at the Battle of Tours and Poitiers, and forced an eventual retreat into Spain. But the Muslim foothold in Andalusia (southern Spain) was firm and endured for nearly eight centuries.

The very year the Muslims crossed into Spain, far to the east the Umayyad armies had conquered Sind in present-day Pakistan. The eastern campaign had consolidated earlier gains in Persia and moved further into Central Asia to what is now Afghanistan. Muslim armies stood near the northwestern quarter of present-day India, but it would be several centuries before Islam would become a presence in India proper. Most importantly, the process of Islamization was well under way in ancient urban centers of west and central Asia such as Samarqand and Bukhara along the Great Silk Road.

Meanwhile, buoyed by their capture of Sicily and the historic city of Chalcedon in Asia Minor, the Umayyads laid a protracted but unsuccessful siege to Constantinople. Surviving yet another Umayyad attack thirty years later, that city would stand firm until it finally fell in 1453. The first great Muslim dynasty had made extraordinary gains in one of the most spectacular three-front advances ever mounted. However, the rapidity of military conquest and expansive political domination should not lead one to conclude that suddenly the whole of the known world had converted to Islam. It was not primarily missionary zeal that motivated

19

the troops, but the promise of adventure and booty. That is not to say that their leaders entirely avoided the rhetoric of heavenly reward for bringing the world into the embrace of Islam. But on the whole, desire for conversion was secondary at best. In fact the Umayyads established a system of taxation under which non-Muslims paid a revenue over and above that expected of Muslims; while this may have encouraged non-Muslims to convert for financial reasons, it gave the conquerors a like incentive to leave the subject peoples a measure of religious liberty.

12. How did the early Muslim administrations deal with non-Muslim subjects? Did they allow freedom of religion?

Under the Umayyads, Muslim rule developed a policy begun under Umar that defined the socioreligious category of *dhimmi* (also *ahl adh-dhimma,* "protected minority"). Non-Muslims who chose not to convert enjoyed basic rights and freedom of worship so long as they paid a "poll tax" *(jizya)* in addition to the universally levied land tax *(kharaj).* The poll tax was a carry-over from both Roman and Sasanian practice. In addition, Muslims were required to pay the *zakat,* legally prescribed alms, one of the "five pillars," while non-Muslims were not. For legal purposes this protected status meant that Jews and Christians were answerable to their own religions' jurisdictions rather than to Islamic religious law. In the Iranian territories, the dhimmis included Zoroastrians as well, and eventually even Hindus were brought under the umbrella of dhimmitude because they possessed their own sacred scriptures.

Non-Muslims were—and still are in some places—under a number of significant restrictions. They were forbidden to proselytize and had to wear clothing that identified their confessional membership. They could repair their ritual sites but could not build new ones, and could not ride horses or bear arms. In some historical settings the restrictions were enforced onerously, but in many cases dhimmis enjoyed considerable latitude. Dhimmis were distinguished from idolaters, who were indeed treated without religious toleration and were left with the choice of fleeing, converting, or fearing for their lives. Jews and Christians did not enjoy what we would consider wide open religious freedom under Islamic rule. Even so, it was in general a far better state of affairs than what Jews or even Christian minority groups often experienced at the hands of majority Christian regimes such as the Byzantine or Spanish Catholic.

13. After such a spectacular beginning, why did the first major dynasty last less than a century?

Amazing as the Umayyad dynasty was in so many ways, it suffered an untimely demise because it ultimately failed to contend with a number of social, religious, and political constituencies. The players in the drama of the fall of the Umayyad dynasty represent a fascinating cross-section of religious interests that have remained alive virtually throughout Islamic history in some form or another. First, the Umayyads came to power largely as a result of their Meccan connections and were thus associated with a kind of Arab aristocracy. As the Muslim sphere expanded, however, the status of non-Arabs who chose to convert to Islam soon became a thorny issue. As a class they were known as "clients" *(mawali),* and as such did not quite enjoy equality with Arab Muslims. According to some sources, Ali and the Shi'a rejected such ethnic distinctions, thus winning the allegiance of some of the *mawali* and reinforcing their discontent with the Umayyads.

Meanwhile, animosity was growing between the Umayyads and the Shi'a, those who had supported the caliphate of Ali. Problems dated back at least to the suspicion that Ali had been involved in the murder of the third caliph, Uthman, who belonged to the Umayyad clan. But in 680 Shi'a-Umayyad relations degenerated still further. Ali's son Husayn decided to press his claim to rule by marching a small armed band out to meet the troops of the Umayyad caliph Yazid. The Umayyad army slaughtered the badly outnumbered Shi'a entourage at Karbala, just south of Baghdad, and in the process made Husayn the Shi'i protomartyr.

Still another faction had earlier separated from the Shi'a and was becoming a thorn in the side of the Umayyads. When Ali had battled the original Umayyad governor of Syria, Mu'awiya, to establish his legitimacy as fourth caliph in 657, the two sides fought to an apparent draw. At that point Ali decided to submit the case to human arbitration, inciting the ire of a group who insisted that they should let God decide through appeal to the Qur'an alone. In anger they decided to withdraw their support and came to be known as the "Seceders" *(khawarij,* pl. of *khariji,* "those who secede"). The Kharijites argued a hard line on membership in the community, claiming only nonsinners were true Muslims. They would come to regard the Umayyads as godless rulers, and hence as un-Muslim and unfit to lead.

In their military operations, the Umayyads had always depended on Arab tribal forces. But that in turn meant choosing sides between traditionally implacable enemies, the northern Qays tribes and the southern Kalb tribes. Opting to bring the Qays with them to Damascus, the Umayyads earned the undying enmity of the Kalb forces then encamped in the garrison towns of Iraq. One of those garrisons was Kufa, a stronghold of the Shi'a; another was Basra, a stronghold of the Khawarij. In such places discontent fed on itself.

Medina, meanwhile, remained the home of prophetic tradition and of religionists convinced they had inherited the custody of Muhammad's authentic legacy. They looked on the Umayyads with suspicion and shared the view of other groups that the rulers were religiously unfit. So, for very different reasons, did small but increasingly important groups of ascetics. From their perspective, the Umayyads had assumed the mantle of royalty and adopted a lifestyle utterly incompatible with the simplicity they associated with Muhammad's example.

Add to this volatile mix a new group of claimants to authority, and the die was cast for the Umayyads. The Abbasids, a faction that traced its lineage to an uncle of Muhammad's named Abbas, now emerged to take advantage of the internal strife. Using a network of propagandists spread across the impossibly far-flung Umayyad realm, the Abbasids united enough of the disaffected parties to eventually undermine the caliphate. By the mid-740s, the Umayyad caliphate was doomed, and in 750 the Abbasids stepped in to inaugurate a regime that would last at least nominally for over five centuries.

14. What other significant divisions developed in the expanding Muslim community?

Major differences between what evolved into the two largest segments of Shi'ites began to crystallize around the second half of the eighth century. Until that time, Shi'i Muslims were in general agreement in recognizing the leadership authority of a hereditary succession of six descendants of Muhammad, beginning with Ali and his two sons, Hasan and Husayn. These figures they called Imams. In 765 C.E., Ja'far as-Sadiq, the sixth in that line, died. Again opinion divided over legitimacy of succession. One group had pledged allegiance to Ja'far's older son, Isma'il. When Isma'il died even before his father did, those who had acknowledged Isma'il's succession continued to insist on its validity. Effectively terminating the line with Isma'il, whose death they interpreted as a temporary departure from the scene, this group came to be called the "Seveners" or "Isma'ilis." They in turn eventually divided into more than one subgroup. Seveners today live, for example, in East Africa, Pakistan, and India. The largest of the groups acknowledges the Aga Khan as its leader.

According to another interpretation of the events of the 760s, Ja'far the Sixth Imam saw fit to abrogate the designation of the deceased Isma'il by naming a younger son, Musa, as his successor. Those who acknowledged Musa's leadership followed a line of succession all the way to a twelfth Imam. Their theological interpretation of history says that in about 874 C.E., the twelfth Imam went into a "lesser concealment," a period during which he communicated to his followers through a series of four representatives *(wakil)*. In 940 C.E., the last of those spokespersons died without having appointed a successor. Since the Imam was no longer actively communicating, Twelver Shi'ites call that date the beginning of the "greater concealment," a condition that obtains to this day. These Twelvers, also called Imamis or Ja'faris, constitute by far the largest Shi'ite group and account for over ninety percent of Iran's population and just over half the population of Iraq. Twelver Shi'ism became the state religion of Iran in the early sixteenth century.

Both Twelver and Sevener views of history are distinctly millennialist in tone. Though there are some important differences in how they have elaborated their theologies, both have historically looked forward to the return or reemergence of the last (i.e., seventh or twelfth) Imam. He will then establish an age of justice in which all believers will reap the rewards of the redemptive suffering of the Imam's extended family (especially for Twelvers) or from the Imam's healing arcane knowledge (a classical Sevener notion). Sunni tradition also looks forward to the advent of a Mahdi (Guided One) at the end of time, but there the idea is not so fundamental as in Shi'i tradition.

15. Christians in Europe during the fifteenth and sixteenth centuries often referred to Christendom's chief rival as "the infidel Turk." Who are the Turks?

When St. Ignatius Loyola, founder of the Society of Jesus, thought of what he could do for the church of his day, toward the top of his list was the desire to convert "the Turk." He and many other devout Catholics would have liked nothing more than to make pilgrimage to the Holy Land, then in the hands of the Ottoman Empire. The story of how the people called Turks came to dominate nearly the whole of the Mediterranean world—and all of western Islamdom—is intriguing and a fine example of the dynamic quality of the history of Islam.

It all started in the ninth century, when conquering Muslim armies in Central Asia began a policy of transporting young prisoners of Turkic origin back to Baghdad and other major cities to serve as palace guards. Caliphs could easily make enemies even among family and friends, and found it necessary to employ "outsiders" who were more capable of disinterested service. Thus was born a class of people within Islamic societies, the Turkish slave soldier.

From time to time the Turkish guard would rise up and take temporary control of the reins in Baghdad. On several occasions promising members of the guard worked their way up through the ranks and were even appointed to high offices in provincial posts. Some took the next logical step, declaring themselves independent rulers when the caliph back in Baghdad had too much on his mind to attend to the provinces.

But the most important train of events began in the late tenth and early eleventh centuries in Central Asia, the ancestral home of the Turks, when a Turkic clan called the Saljuqids converted to Islam. These new Sunni Muslims consolidated their power in Central Asia, and in 1055 had taken Baghdad and established the Sultanate as a temporal institution parallel to the Caliphate, which they had reduced largely to a position of spiritual leadership. From there the Saljuqid rulers launched campaigns northward against the eastern frontier of the Byzantine Empire. In 1071 the Turks defeated a Byzantine force in eastern Anatolia—after which a call for help went out to Rome, resulting in the first Crusade in 1096. But the Saljuqids, now joined by other Turkic groups on the march into Anatolia, continued to push westward, squeezing the Byzantines back toward Constantinople. By the late thirteenth century, another Turkic clan led by Osman was gathering support from other Turkic groups, and emerged as the leading military power. Osman's confederation was the beginning of what would become the Ottoman Empire, renaming the Byzantine capital Istanbul after capturing it in 1453. At its height the Ottoman realm was one of the largest in history, stretching from the gates of Vienna across the Balkans, from the Caucasus to the Yemen, and from Alexandria to Algeria. Ottoman sultans generally conceived of themselves as supreme rulers of all Muslims, even if they did not claim the title of caliph. The Empire gave way to the Turkish Republic under Kemal Ataturk in the 1920s.

16. How did the Muslim leaders administer the vast territories they conquered? Did they impose their own law on everyone they subjugated?

At various times in Islamic history different models of leadership have predominated. By far the single most important has been that of the Caliphate. In that model, the successor to the Prophet, the Caliph, has ideally served as both political and spiritual leader, Commander of the Army and of the Faithful. After the Caliphate's beginning in Medina and reestablishment for some eighty-nine years in Damascus, it moved to Baghdad for some five centuries; but the caliphate's authority did not go uncontested. Several rival caliphates laid claims, most notably in Cordoba and Cairo (under an Isma'ili Shi'i dynasty called the Fatimids). In the mid-eleventh century the Caliphate suffered a severe abridgment when Turkic Saljuqids overcame Baghdad and vested the caliph's temporal power in a new parallel institution called the Sultanate. After the Mongols sacked Baghdad in 1258, various dynasties made largely symbolic attempts to prop up or otherwise revive the moribund institution. Nowadays the caliphate is a memory, though some still dream of its resurgence.

In addition, claimants to leadership of the Imamate type arose from time to time. Mahdist movements (Sunni groups that focus on the return of a divinely "guided" person called the Mahdi) have been attempted with varying degrees of success until modern times. One abortive attempt at such a movement occurred as recently as 1979, around the beginning of the Iranian revolution and the storming of the American embassy in Tehran. At that time Sunni and Shi'i Muslims alike were observing the beginning of the fifteenth Islamic century. In Tehran Twelver Shi'ites relived the suffering of Husayn against the evil tyrant in their struggle against the evil Shah and the United States in regular observances that mark the beginning of every year, but take on renewed importance at the turn of a century. In Mecca a small Mahdist group, recalling the tradition that with each new century God would raise up for Islam a "renewer," took over the sanctuary of the Ka'ba and proclaimed a short-lived new age, but paid with their lives for daring to violate the holy place.

Fully developed theologies of succession, and theories regarding the religious and genealogical qualifications of a ruler did not appear for several centuries because the separate identities of Sunni and Shi'i groups evolved rather gradually. The divergence of views that began in the earliest years, however, led to a variety of theoretical justifications on both sides of the issue.

17. People sometimes characterize Islam as an uncivilized or "desert" religion. Is this an accurate assessment?

Step back to the year 1000 and imagine yourself traveling across the Mediterranean world from east to west, beginning in Baghdad, and you will find yourself treated to an array of splendid world-class cities you may never have dreamed existed. Though India and China, along with Central and South America, boasted many of the world's finest cities, virtually the only non-Muslim city in the greater Mediterranean worth a second look at the time was Constantinople. London and Paris were still little more than towns.

Baghdad was founded in 762 as the new capital of the Abbasid dynasty. The caliph designed it as a perfect circle with the palace and its mosque at the center, its surrounding walls reserving places for representatives of virtually every segment of society within Islamdom. Obviously an idealized structure, the original design did not last long because of rapid expansion. Still, in the mid-eleventh century, Baghdad was an important center of learning and culture. By 1100 the city boasted some of the premier intellectual institutions in the world.

Further to the west was the city of Cairo, founded in 969 by a Sevener Shi'i dynasty called the Fatimids. A century into its history Cairo was booming, a center of trade, culture, and learning. There in 972 the al-Azhar mosque was founded, the forerunner of what would become one of the world's oldest institutions of higher learning. Portions of the fortified wall of the old Fatimid city of Cairo still stand in testimony to its medieval glory.

Moving further west, one finds a number of important urban centers, from Qayrawan in present-day Tunisia, to Fez in Morocco. Founded as a garrison town in 670, Qayrawan grew into one of several important North African centers of learning. Fez originated about a century later and, along with Marrakesh (founded 1070), was at or near the center of several Moroccan Arab and Berber dynasties over the subsequent six centuries.

Arguably the most splendid city in Western Europe in the year 1000 was the Andalusian jewel called Cordoba. Founded in early Roman times, it passed from the Romans to the Vandals to the Byzantines and back to the Visigoths. With the Muslim occupation of Cordoba in 711, what had been a minor, lackluster town began its steady four-century rise to prominence. Some of the great monuments of Islamic Cordoba remain a major attraction to travelers today. As the scene of remarkable symbiosis of the three Abrahamic faiths for several hundred years, a *"convivencia"* of Judaism, Christianity, and Islam, two of Cordoba's most famous citizens were Ibn Rushd (a.k.a. Averroes, d. 1198) and Maimonides (d. 1204).

18. Islam was once prominent in Spain. How did it become so important there, and what happened to the Muslims of Spain?

Beginning with the initial conquests after the Muslim armies crossed the straits of Gibraltar in 711, an important Arab Islamic presence established itself in Spain within fifty years or so. After the fall of the Umayyad dynasty in Damascus, the incoming Abbasids tried to eliminate the last of the royal house's descendants. One prince managed to escape to

Spain, there to establish the Umayyad Emirate of Cordoba. Later it would grow into the Cordoba Caliphate to challenge Baghdad's authority.

Spain's population had become latinized over the preceding eight centuries or more. Jews who had lived in the Iberian peninsula since Roman times experienced considerable persecution under the Christian rulers and were among the first to taste the benefits of the Arab Muslim conquest: they were given their religious freedom, while members of the Christian population were allowed to retain their Roman institutional heritage as a basis for local order. As for larger political and cultural traditions, the Arabs drew heavily on their Middle Eastern roots. Educated Christians and Jews learned Arabic widely, and Middle Eastern taste in fashions, luxury items, art, and architecture found ready acceptance. The over seven-hundred-year presence of Islam in Spain also left a lasting influence on the Spanish language. The expression of enthusiastic approval, *Ole!*, comes from the Arabic *Wa 'llahi,* "By God!"; and dozens of Spanish words that begin with *al-,* such as *almohada* which both in Spanish and Arabic refers to a pillow, are evidence of that influence.

The Catholic reconquest of Spain gradually reclaimed important Muslim cities—Toledo (1085), Cordoba (1236), and Seville (1248), with only the Nasrid kingdom in Granada holding out until 1492. Determined to purge the land of any taint of infidel faith, Ferdinand and Isabella gave remaining Muslims and Jews the choice of conversion, exile, or death. Muslim converts to Christianity, called Moriscos, continued to live in small communities, but after 1500 Spanish Islam was little more than a memory. Today some Muslims are emigrating to Spain from North Africa, though in much smaller numbers than to France.

19. I know there are many Muslims in the Indian subcontinent, an area once considered a single entity and now split into Pakistan, India, and Bangladesh. How did Islam develop there?

Early conquests brought Islam to the region of Sind, in present-day Pakistan, by 711. Over the next several centuries a succession of Muslim dynasties made occasional advances into the Punjab in north-western India. In 1191 the Ghurid dynasty captured Delhi and established the first major Muslim presence in the heart of India and became the first of a succession of Sultanates to hold sway in various regions of the subcontinent. The most important of these was that of Tughluq Shah (1320–51), who managed to unite most of northern and central India from Delhi. For the next sixty years or so the Tughluqids shared power with several other dynasties that ruled to the south, while the kings of Bengal established their independent rule over a newly Islamized population. In 1526 Babur conquered Delhi and established the Mughal dynasty, whose rule would soon encompass most of the subcontinent. Babur's grandson Akbar (r. 1556–1605) was the patron of major cultural and religious developments effected through a vast network of international relations. Akbar's son Jahangir (r. 1605–27) and grandson Shah Jahan (r. 1628–57) continued to rule in splendor. They constructed some of the world's finest architectural creations, including the Taj Mahal, in which Shah Jahan and his wife are buried. Akbar's great grandson Awrangzib (1658–1707) was less tolerant of religious pluralism and presided over the beginning of the end of Mughal glory.

Today the Indian subcontinent is home to nearly one-third of the world's Muslims. In 1948 the state of Pakistan was partitioned from India as a Muslim state. In 1971 East Pakistan gained its independence under the name Bangladesh. Pakistan and Bangladesh are almost entirely Muslim, while the Muslim population of India constitutes the world's largest Islamic minority.

20. Most of the people in China's western province of Xinjiang are Muslims. How did Islam get to China? Are there any distinctively Chinese features of their Islam?

Approximately twenty million citizens, perhaps more, of the Peoples' Republic of China consider themselves Muslims. Fully ten different "nationalities" make up the entire Muslim population, but about half of that total belong to the Hui people. The Hui resemble the majority Han population in physical appearance, and they speak Chinese (unlike the other Muslim minorities, several of which speak Turkic languages). But the Hui think of themselves as a distinct people in that they disavow ancestor veneration, gambling, drinking, and eating pork. Many Chinese mosques are built in distinctively Chinese architectural styles. Their minarets are square rather than cylindrical and have the gracefully curved roofing associated with the pagoda.

According to ancient tradition, Islam came to China in the seventh century with Arab silk merchants. In the mid-eighth century an Abbasid caliph dispatched a regiment of Turkic soldiers to help the Chinese emperor put down the revolt of a mutinous officer. Remaining after the war, those soldiers formed the nucleus of inland Muslim communities. Over the next four centuries the Muslim population grew very slowly in coastal and central regions. But in 1215 Genghis Khan's Mongols captured Beijing and eventually overthrew the Sung Dynasty. Under the Yuan (Mongol) dynasty the Muslims enjoyed privileged status. Meanwhile, various segments of the population in the northwestern province of Xinjiang converted to Islam. After the Yuan dynasty fell to the Ming (1368–1644), Muslim fortunes took a turn for the worse, and under the Manchu dynasty (1644–1911) they endured several centuries of persecution. During Mao's Cultural Revolution the Muslims suffered terribly again, but have regained many important rights during the past fifteen years or so.

THREE:

BELIEFS AND PRACTICES

21. What are the "Five Pillars" of Islam? Are they a good summary of the basic beliefs and practices enjoined on all Muslims?

Virtually every summary of Islamic belief and practice begins with the notion of the "five pillars," a convenient device for remembering the basics, so long as one keeps in mind that they represent minimum religious obligations and are thus only part of a much larger reality. The first is the profession of belief *(shahada),* a deceptively simple affirmation that "There is no deity but God and Muhammad is the Messenger of God." In the profession are hidden all the nuances of faith in a God who is pure oneness and otherness, and of reliance on the veracity of the human means by which God has chosen to become known, namely, the succession of prophets of whom Muhammad is the last.

The second pillar is the observance of five brief but regular ritual prayer times that mark off sacred moments throughout each day, from early morning to late evening. One can perform the ritual prayer *(salat)* anywhere; the only spatial requirement is a physical orientation toward the Arabian city of Mecca, home of the ancient shrine of the Ka'ba. Water, a universal symbol of cleansing, provides the physical medium for Muslims as they wash before the five daily prayers. The tradition makes it clear that the purification is at least as much spiritual as it is bodily; if water is not available, one can use sand or even earth to wipe over the feet, forearms, and face. The requirements are thus far from literalistic. Purification functions primarily as an embodiment of the praying person's movement into a sacred time.

If the profession of faith and ritual prayer call for daily, if not constant, awareness, the practice of the remaining three pillars, almsgiving, fasting, and pilgrimage, is more occasional. Islam's strong sense of social awareness recommends that Muslims be at all times as generous as possible to the needy through charitable gifts (called *sadaqa*). Almsgiving *(zakat),* strictly speaking, resembles a tax with a more formal legal aspect in that tradition stipulates who is required to give *zakat* and

33

from what kinds of resources. Again and again the Qur'an refers favor-
ably to those "who perform the ritual prayer and provide alms," linking
the two practices as though the one looked to the individual's spiritual
welfare and the other to the larger community's external well-being. A
central Muslim belief is that one's wealth and possessions are temporary; they are merely on loan. Muslim tradition recommends that
believers "give God a loan" and "spend in the way of God" as a way of
caring for creation and sharing what they have received. The term *zakat*
comes from a root that means "to purify oneself," in this case, of the
delusion of ownership. God alone is substantially and eternally wealthy.
The point of giving alms, like that of fasting, is to remind the donor of
the source of all good gifts.

Almost all religious traditions recommend fasting in some form
or other, but Islamic practice retains a particularly rigorous version of
the seasonal fast during the ninth lunar month of Ramadan. Abstain-
ing from food, drink, and sexual gratification from dawn to sunset
every day (sometimes as long as eighteen hours or more when
Ramadan falls in summertime) for thirty days breaks the ordinary
pattern of daily living as a sharp reminder to focus on the more
important dimensions of life. Refraining from ordinary recourse to
creation's sustenance reminds one of a greater need that only God
can fill. Not alone from physical goods does one fast, but from a
range of physical and spiritual evils as well, including envy and
hatred, and lesser faults like complaining or cutting corners in one's
work. Among the desired effects of the practice Muslims count a
deepened compassion for the poor and hungry, a heightened capacity
to counter one's own baser tendencies, and a clearer sense of one's
relationship to the Creator.

Finally, pilgrimage. Of all the world's religious traditions, none
has maintained so strong a sense of its members as a community on pilgrimage as has the Islamic tradition. Given good health and sufficient
means, Muslims are enjoined to visit Mecca at least once in a lifetime
during the sacred time of pilgrimage, the Hajj. Muslims are welcomed
to Mecca and Medina any time during the year, but fulfill formally the
duty of Hajj only between the eighth and thirteenth days of the twelfth
lunar month.

22. You mentioned that the *shahada* is "deceptively simple." How so?

With the first half of the profession, "There is no deity but God," Muslims acknowledge the unity, uniqueness, and transcendence of God. This is about as pure and unvarnished a statement of religious focus as one can imagine, demanding of believers uncompromising discipline and vigilance over their affections and spiritual loyalties. It calls believers to the lifelong project of sensitivity to all the subtle forms of idolatry to which human beings are susceptible. No one exemplifies dedication to that project better than the prophet Abraham in the Qur'an's account of how he severed his ties to home and family in search of a new direction in life. One night, the scripture says, Abraham beheld a star and said, "This is my Lord." But when the star soon disappeared, he confessed, "I love not things that set." When the moon rose, Abraham exclaimed, "This must be my Lord." But when it, too, set, he said, "Were not my Lord guiding me, I would surely be among the lost." And when he saw the sun come up he said, "This must indeed by my Lord, for it is greater by far." But when the sun went down, Abraham addressed his father's people: "Far be it from me to set up partners with God as you do."

In the following verse, the Qur'an has Abraham say the words every Muslim says at the start of the ritual prayer as they face Mecca: "I have turned my face toward Him who created heavens and earth [i.e., not to created nature itself], as a seeker after the One God, in grateful surrender [literally as a *hanif* and a *muslim*], and I worship none but God" (Qur'an 6:76–79). Abraham could face the true center of life only after he had eliminated all that could compete for his attention. Abraham was reading what the Qur'an calls the "signs on the horizons" for what they reveal of God. Speaking of those who reject that self-discipline, the Qur'an says (God speaking): "I will turn away from my signs those who walk proudly on earth. Though they see every sign, they will put no credence in them. Though they may see the way of uprightness they will not set out upon it. Should they see the errant way, that they will claim as theirs; for they denied and refused to attend to our signs" (Qur'an 7:146).

Here is the deepest meaning of the terms "islam" and "muslim." The Arabic root *S-L-M* carries the connotation of being in that state of

wholeness and balance that results from having all of one's relationships and priorities in order. That state is called *SaLaM* (related to the
Hebrew *shalom*). Now when a person pursues that state in relation to
God, it means attributing to God and to none else what belongs to God,
and that is the root meaning of *iSLaM*. One who achieves that state of
propriety in relation to God is a *muSLiM;* literally, "one brings about a
state of *SaLaM*" by acknowledging that God alone, to follow up on the
imagery of Abraham's story, "does not set."

23. What do Muslims mean by the term "Allah"; is this deity anything like what Christians and Jews mean by the term "God"?

Many non-Muslims have the impression that the term Allah
refers to some despotic deity with a taste for violence and infidel
blood. Perhaps that is because so many television and movie images
of Muslim soldiers depict them screaming *"Allahu Akbar"* (God is
supreme) as they attack or celebrate victory. How is it, many wonder,
that they seem so readily to associate Allah with violence? In Arabic,
the word *Allah* is simply a compound of *al-* (the definite article, "the")
and *ilah* (god, deity). Joined together, they signify "God." Nearly all
Arabic speakers, including Jews and Christians, refer to their Supreme
Being as Allah.

Most Jews and Christians are convinced that their God is loving
and kind, provident and generous, as well as thirsty for justice and
equity. So are most Muslims. Of the "Ninety-Nine Most Beautiful
Names" of God, the two by far most frequently invoked are "Gracious
or Compassionate" and "Merciful." All but one of the Qur'an's 114
suras begin with the phrase, "In the name of God, the Compassionate
and Merciful...." One might say these two names are as important for
Muslims as are the names *Father, Son,* and *Holy Spirit,* heard in so
many Christian invocations. Virtually every Muslim public speaker
begins with that Qur'anic phrase, and goes on to wish the audience the
blessings and mercy of God.

The opening chapter of the Qur'an sets the tone of prayer for
Muslims and lays the foundation for our present consideration:

> In the Name of God, the Compassionate and Merciful:
> Praise to God, Lord of the Universe.

The Compassionate, the Merciful,
Master of the Day of Judgment.
You alone do we serve; from you alone do we seek help.
Lead us along the Straight Path,
the path of those who experience the shower of your grace,
not of those who have merited your anger
or of those who have gone astray. (Qur'an 1:1–7)

Here one finds clues to several of the principal divine attributes. Compassion and mercy top the list and receive an emphatic second mention. In addition, God rules the "two worlds" (seen and unseen, i.e., the universe), takes account at Judgment, offers aid and grace, and manifests a wrathful side to those who prefer arrogant independence from the Origin of all things. Not one of the Ninety-Nine Names of God, on which Muslims meditate as they finger the thirty-three beads of the rosary, will sound a dissonant note in the ear of Christian or Jew.

All of the names conjure up divine attributes which Islamic tradition has divided into those that express God's beauty and approachability *(jamal),* and those that evoke the divine majesty and awe-inspiring power *(jalal).* These references to the two sides of God recall the theological distinction between immanence and transcendence. God is both near and accessible—closer even than the jugular vein, according to Qur'an 50:16—and infinitely beyond human experience and imagining. In the final analysis, many of the images Muslims have of God are very much like those Jews and Christians have.

24. What about the second half of the *shahada,* the part about Muhammad?

"I confess that Muhammad is the Messenger of God" sums up what Muslims believe about the human need for guidance and about how God has provided assistance through a succession of prophets. Muhammad is, of course, not the only messenger of God, but he is the last. In his definitive communication of God's word, Muslims see the corrective needed because of earlier misunderstandings and willful corruption of revelation delivered through previous prophets. Muhammad's message is not new. It reaffirms the truth of the original revelation brought by

Moses, David, and Jesus. It differs from the earlier prophetic messages
only in that God has chosen now to reveal the Word in Arabic. Islamic
tradition names earlier Arabian prophets such as Hud, Salih, and
Shu'ayb; but none of them brought a scriptural message and none was
sent with a universal revelation. They were prophets *(nabi)*, but not messengers *(rasul)*.

25. Muslims believe God reveals through the Qur'an and that Muhammad's own sayings expand on the scripture. Are there any other means of revelation?

One of the Qur'an's most beautiful images suggests that there is
more to God's revelation than even the scripture can contain: "If all the
trees on the earth were pens, and all the oceans ink, and seven times
that, they would not be able to record the words of God" (31:27; see also
18:109). Islamic tradition also sees important dimensions of divine disclosure in God's work as Creator, both of nature broadly conceived and
of the individual human being. The Qur'an speaks of "signs" on the
"horizons" and within the "self" (Qur'an 41:53; 51:20–21). "Behold, in
the heavens and the earth are signs for those who believe. And in your
creation, and all the wild creatures He has scattered over the earth, are
signs for a people of firm faith. And the alternation of night and day,
and the sustenance that God sends down from the sky, to revive the
earth after its death, and the shifting of the winds—these are signs for a
people who understand....Here is vision for humankind, guidance and
mercy...." (Qur'an 45:3–5, 20).

Mention of God's handiwork occurs often in the Qur'an as the
first, if the not the foremost, locus of divine revelation. Anyone who
sees the natural world in all its wonder with open eyes and an open heart
will see there the unmistakable signs of the Creator. But the difference
between God and creation is infinite; one discerns divinity *through*
nature rather than precisely in nature. A "Sacred Hadith," a tradition
attributed to God rather than to Muhammad, says: "I was a hidden trea-
sure and I desired to be known, so I created the world." Knowing God
through that world renders all created beings naturally "muslim," for all
nonhuman things by nature surrender to God. As the Qur'an says, "Do
you not see that it is God whom all in heaven and on earth, and the birds

in formation, praise? Every being knows its proper prayer and praise" (Qur'an 24:41, with the word for "prayer" being *salat,* the technical term for ritual prayer). Only human beings have to choose whether they will prefer self-centeredness and the illusion of control.

God also reveals by means of "signs" within the individual person, but the tradition does not call God's disclosure in this instance "revelation." Instead, God casts into the heart a "light" that illuminates the individual's relationship to God. Scriptural verses such as "Wherever you turn, there is the face of God" (2:109), and "We [God] are closer to the person than the jugular vein" (50:16) convey a sense of God's nearness. The same sentiment occurs in sayings of Muhammad such as "Who knows oneself knows one's Lord," and in the Sacred Hadiths: "I fulfill my servant's expectations of Me," and "Though the heavens and the earth cannot contain Me, there is room for Me in the believer's heart."

26. Do Muslims believe in angels?

Belief in angels is among the basic elements included in the extended creedal statements in the Qur'an that speak of God's prophets, books, and the last day. Several angels are mentioned in the Qur'an, but Gabriel is the most prominent. His role is that of delivering God's message to prophets. Michael's task is to supply sustenance to human bodies and knowledge to minds. The angel Israfil will sound the final trumpet at Judgment, but meanwhile is entrusted with ensouling bodies and relaying God's orders to Michael. In addition there are innumerable anonymous angels who move among the levels of the heavenly realm and between heaven and earth. To each person two guardian angels are assigned, and there is much charming lore about the spiritual services these angels render. Other angels busy themselves ferrying blessings down to believers and bringing back to heaven word about the good things the believers are doing. To Azrael, the angel of death, falls the task of visiting each person whose time is at hand. Angels function in Islamic theology and tradition very much as they do in Christian thought: they represent an intermediary personal presence that embodies divine interest in the affairs of God's creatures.

27. What do Muslims believe about the "last things"—death, judgment, heaven, hell? Is their eschatology at all similar to that of Christianity?

Many features of Islamic eschatology will remind Christians of their own tradition's views of death, judgment, heaven, and hell. Nearly all of the Qur'an's many references to death refer at least indirectly to the omnipotence of the God who "Brings to life" and "Causes to die" (two of the ninety-nine names). One of the earliest references relates directly to the content of Muhammad's preaching and the refusal of his listeners to accept it: they have committed spiritual suicide. All unbelief amounts to inner death. Unbelievers scoff and insist they will suffer only the "first death" of the body when their predetermined span of life is over.

Most of the relevant texts concern physical life and death in relation to God's power. As exhortatory devices in Muhammad's preaching, they remind that God's absolute dominion over life and death can give the believer unshakable confidence. God's purposeful control over life span, as opposed to the arbitrary and despotic control the pre-Islamic Arabs had attributed to impersonal "Time" or "Fate," leaves the believer free to attend to life as it happens, in the conviction that life is not pure chance but part of a great design. God's providence gives the believer hope in the resurrection, for God will not suffer creation to come to naught.

Every major creedal statement formulated by the early theologians includes statements about death, and specifically about the "punishment of the tomb" and the angelic interrogators who question the deceased about their lives and deeds. Both features seem to arise from Hadiths suggesting that the dead retain their perceptive faculties. According to one creed, body and soul are reunited in the tomb; infidels will surely suffer there, and believers who have sinned may also suffer. In any case, even the obedient believer will experience the "pressure" of the tomb. But, according to a Hadith, no punishment will be inflicted on a Muslim who dies on Friday, and the pressure will last only an hour. The Qur'an mentions neither the interrogating angels, Munkar and Nakir, nor the pressure and punishment of the grave. These traditional elements gradually became more detailed and embellished, and have become, to some degree, articles of faith.

Some sayings of the Prophet about death are blatantly contradictory. Weep for the dead; do not weep for them; weep for only one day;

weep for an extended period; the more you weep the more suffering the dead will feel from the pain of separation; weep to help them with your sympathy; and so forth. What is important here is simply that tradition attributes to the Prophet the complete range of responses to death and mortality.

All will be held accountable for their deeds at Judgment. A number of Hadiths are as much instructions on how to live as on how to die. "Die before you die," the Prophet advises; let preoccupation with self pass away now, so that when death comes you will have handed over already that which you fear most to lose. "As you live, so shall you die; and as you die, so shall you be raised up." Therefore, leave your good deeds behind when you go and your good deeds will be your traveling companions on your journey after death.

After the resurrection of the body, everyone will experience either reward or punishment, heaven or hell. There is no Purgatory as such, but the passageway between this life and the next, called the *barzakh,* could be considered a rough analogy. In addition, some hold that a temporary stay in hell serves that function. Many of the Meccans to whom Muhammad preached scoffed at his teaching of the "second death" of eternal damnation. The Qur'an insists that in the Fire one neither lives nor dies; all who end up there will beg for death. The Qur'an's imagery of the double death is very similar to that of some early Christian literature.

For those who have spent a life of faith and good works, eternal reward awaits. As in many other traditions, the scriptural imagery of paradise describes heaven as a realm of endless pleasures. Many Muslims understand the imagery in its widest sense to refer to a state of delight that results from being forever in God's presence.

28. Muslims often use the expression *"In sha' Allah,"* which means (more or less) "God willing" or "If God wishes." Is this connected to the "fatalism" popularly associated with Islam?

Many Muslims believe that an uncompromising form of predestination is a central tenet of Islamic theology. And it is true that even in the classic creedal formulations elaborated as far back as the eighth and ninth centuries, one finds cryptic expressions such as "What hits you could not have missed you, and what misses you could not have hit you." Many people take that to mean that one's lot or destiny is set in stone from all eternity, and the individual human being is powerless to alter that course. It is important to note the context in which such expressions originally occurred. One of the first theological issues to which Muslims addressed themselves arose in connection with political responsibility: is a leader fully responsible for his actions, and if so, should subjects rise up and overthrow a ruler who is behaving in ways inconsistent with Islamic values? In the case of some of the early creeds, it seems clear that some theorists virtually excused the wickedness of some rulers in order to avoid social upheaval. Better to keep a reprehensible ruler than to risk chaos, they argued in effect. Majority opinion among Muslim thinkers has generally emphasized God's absolute power while paying less attention to what their statements implied about human beings.

Numerous texts in the Qur'an suggest that God never wrests effective power of self-determination from the individual. "We turn a person whichever way he wants to turn" (Qur'an 4:115 according to Fazlur Rahman's interpretation). "God does not change a people's state until they change what is within themselves" (Qur'an 8:53; see also 13:11). The scripture's insistence on the need to seek forgiveness unceasingly suggests the personal freedom to change.

On balance, however, Muslim ethical thinking has always gotten around to confronting the issue of human responsibility. A saying attributed to Muhammad epitomizes the dilemma beautifully: "One who denies God's decree is an unbeliever, but one who claims never to have sinned is a liar." It expresses vividly the need to live with the paradoxical coexistence of God's absolute control over all affairs and the awareness that each human being remains responsible for every choice and cannot seek refuge in predestination by pleading, "God made me do it."

Throughout Islamic history, but particularly in the early centuries, questions of the relationship between faith and works have been of political as well as theological import. Various opinions developed as to whether, and to what degree, a person known to have sinned could still be considered a Muslim. On one extreme, the Kharijites identified faith with works so completely that they defined religious community as an assembly of the sinless. At the other end of the spectrum was the view that God's predetermination of events was so broad as to exonerate even blatant godlessness, with the important political implication that rulers could do as they pleased and revolution could not be justified. Majority opinion ended up somewhere closer to the middle. With respect to freedom of action, God creates all potential deeds, including evil ones, but leaves human beings the option as to which they will "appropriate" as their own. As for whether one's known choices render a person unfit to be called a Muslim, most would argue that the best position is to leave the ultimate judgment up to God.

Muhammad's saying, "Trust in God but tie your camel," is not unlike a saying attributed to Ignatius Loyola: "Work as if everything depended on you, and pray as if everything depended on God." Both express something of the paradox attendant on believing in the unfathomable mystery of God's omnipotence while acknowledging human responsibility.

29. I've heard that Muslims traditionally consider only handwritten copies of the Qur'an acceptable. But surely there must be printed versions—how do they reconcile that? And what about using computers to study the Qur'an; is that allowed?

Because the Qur'an is considered the actual word of God, the way in which one reproduces it matters a great deal. Since very early in Islamic history, fine calligraphy has been an important dimension of the whole "experience" of the Qur'an for Muslims. An expert calligrapher who is commissioned to produce a copy of the sacred text does not merely sit down and dash it off as though it were just another job. Spiritual preparation is critical, for the act of writing the word of God is itself a devotional act. Inscribing the revealed writ must therefore be kept a human action so far as possible. It is true that Muslim publishers of editions of the Qur'an do not set the text in type the way, for example, a newspaper uses typesetting. However, that does not necessarily mean that every copy of the Qur'an is actually handwritten. Use of lithography, a printing process by which a plate of a handwritten text is used to duplicate the page, has long been common practice.

In the age of computers and CD-ROM's and the various multimedia devices available to students and devout persons, Muslims have worked to preserve a sense of the sacredness of the physical presence of the revealed text. One can now purchase at very reasonable cost software packages that provide on-screen Qur'anic text together with recitation recorded by noted specialists. What appears on the screen is a reproduction of an originally handwritten page, now typically embellished with different colored "inks" and decorative touches. Many of these software packages include not only the Arabic text, but interpretations of it in as many as half a dozen languages that can be displayed along with it, and some even provide selections from classical exegetical commentaries on the Qur'an. Programs such as this also allow detailed searches of key terms, making the careful study of the Qur'an quite easy for those with computers.

30. News reports about events in the Middle East and North Africa often mention Muslim "fundamentalists." Are they similar to fundamentalists in other religious traditions?

Unfortunately the term "fundamentalist" has come to be synonymous with "extremist," at least when it comes to Muslims. More recently, a similar identification has begun to catch up with some right-wing groups of Israeli settlers bent on pressing their case for continued occupation of the West Bank. One has to make several distinctions in the interest of simple fairness. First of all, fundamentalism is not necessarily the same as literalism in the interpretation of religious sources. I would venture to say that a considerable majority of people who consider themselves religiously engaged tend to be "fundamentalists" to the extent that they seek to live according to their traditions' "fundamental" values. Many religious persons, however, are quite sophisticated in their interpretation of the sources of their traditions.

Second, the vast majority of Muslims would say that people who commit violent acts of terrorism have very definitely lost hold of the fundamentals of their faith. Likewise, most Christians admit that people who blow up abortion clinics also have lost hold of the fundamentals of their faith. In short, most Muslims would likely agree that a life based on the fundamentals of Islam cannot embrace extremist behavior.

31. Do Muslims have a specially educated and even ordained clergy entrusted with teaching and governing?

Islam has no ordained clergy as such, though some individuals do pursue special training in religious studies and law for the purposes of scholarship and local leadership in their communities. Those studies emphasize a thorough familiarity with the Qur'an in its original language, Arabic, with the extensive tradition of scriptural exegesis *(tafsir)* and the literature enshrining the sayings of Muhammad, and with the religious law of one of the dominant methodological schools.

Every mosque has an *imam*. In smaller less well-established congregations various members of the community may take their turns in the role. The imam is not ordained but is chosen from among the upright and competent men of the local community to lead the prayer and to preach the Friday sermon. Larger communities frequently have a full-time imam. His responsibilities are in many ways like those of the pastor of a parish church. In addition to leading the main occasions of ritual prayer, the imam instructs young people planning to marry, visits sick members of the congregation, and acts as overall administrator of the foundation. In many cases that may include oversight of a school. Some imams in this country also engage in interreligious activities. Even in larger congregations, other male members of the community will take turns leading the ritual prayer on days when the imam cannot be at the mosque during prayer time.

In the United States and Canada, many communities have sought out their imams from among religious scholars known to their members, or from individuals whose availability for service comes to be known through the "grapevine" or through ads in Islamic publications. Among the most important qualifications of an imam are fluency in both English and Arabic; solid grounding in the religious sciences of Qur'an and Hadith and *fiqh;* knowing the Qur'an by heart and developed skills in recitation; and some administrative and teaching experience. Congregations still sometimes bring in an imam from overseas, since some regard the quality of formal education in religious sciences available in places like Cairo and Saudi Arabia as highly desirable in an imam.

Four:

Law and Ethics

32. Is there an "Islamic Ethic," and if so is it similar to the "Judaeo-Christian ethic"? Do Muslims believe in "original sin"?

People who seek to live out the Judaeo-Christian ethic are actually espousing a Judaeo-Christian-Islamic ethic. Christians and Jews are often shocked when I suggest that Islam's basic ethical teachings are entirely consistent with those of Judaism and Christianity. Their surprise, it turns out, usually arises out of the unfair association of Muslims with violence in news reports on the Middle East. Of course, the *theologies* behind them are both different and distinctive, but the practical ramifications are entirely compatible.

To begin with, Islam, like virtually every major religious tradition, has its version of the "golden rule," enshrined in a saying of Muhammad: "None among you is a believer until he wishes for his brothers and sisters what he wishes for himself." But as in Judaism and Christianity, the fundamental requirements are far more demanding than that. Islamic tradition does not have a "decalogue" as such, but it most definitely demands all of that and more as its "ethical minimum." In fact, the moral injunction to "Command the good and forbid the evil" goes a step further than the saying familiar to Christians, "Do good and avoid evil."

Islam's teachings on sin and final accountability are highly developed. The essential sin is that of forgetfulness of God, the heedlessness that can gradually stifle the voice of conscience until it becomes but a "distant call" (Qur'an 41:44). Forgetfulness of God leads directly to forgetfulness of one's inmost self. Remembrance of God *(dhikr)* effects personal integration and balances the tension between power and powerlessness, hope and despair, knowledge and ignorance, freedom and determinism. Prospects for the individual in Islam are thoroughly positive so long as one grants the need for reverent awe in God's presence, so long as one acknowledges that God's mercy will overcome his wrath. God will burden no person beyond his or her capacity to persevere.

Islam rejects the notions of original sin and redemption because human beings are directly responsible. Adam and Eve sinned, but humankind has not inherited their guilt. No human action makes the slightest personal difference to God; the moral quality of each individual's choices turns on their ultimate benefit to the human race. It is not God, therefore, but the individual who decides his or her own final destiny. Those who make their choices in this life in isolation from the needs of the human community as a whole will fashion their own hell hereafter. Those who delude themselves into thinking that their choices have created mountains will see those choices reduced to a particle of sand. One of the terms the Qur'an frequently uses to describe greed, selfishness, and sinfulness generally, is "going nowhere fast" *(dalal, aimlessness, wandering in error).*

Seeking forgiveness is at the heart of Qur'anic ethics; it is the first step toward becoming receptive to the experience of God's mercy, and hence toward the furtherance of good conduct in grateful response *(islam)* to the signs on the horizons and in the self that are part of God's mercy. In other words, moral growth is an ascending spiral. In conclusion then, it seems clear that the term "Judaeo-Christian-Islamic ethic" is an appropriate one.

33. Do Muslims have a code of religious law like Jewish rabbinical law or Catholic canon law? How did it develop?

The Qur'an contains some explicit regulations regarding matters of personal and social morality as well as ritual practice, but in general the Muslim scripture does not function as a legislative handbook. Very early in Islamic history, local communities faced issues on which the holy book rendered no explicit opinion or ruling. Then as now, the community's most pressing challenge was how to interpret the sacred text so as to preserve its spirit and still respond to changing needs.

While Muhammad lived, problematical issues could be decided by the Prophet's responses and clarifications. Not long after his death, what had begun as a rather informal process of preserving Muhammad's utterances in the living memory of Muslims, evolved into a more formal process. To prevent the loss of prophetic tradition, scholars went in search of Hadith (sayings or traditions) across the world. Collecting massive numbers of them, they sifted through the material, attempting to sort out the authentic from the spurious. By the end of the ninth century, Muhammad's words and deeds had been institutionalized into a number of written collections, six of which have been considered especially authoritative. These collections of Hadith came to form the second major source upon which scholars would base their decisions on the shape of Muslim life.

All Muslims agree on the primacy of the Qur'an as the source of revealed truth, and on the importance of Hadith as the principal source of information about the example of the Prophet, the Sunna. Originally most Muslim scholars considered Sunna virtually coextensive with Hadith: all that one could know, or needed to know, about the Prophet's example, one could find in the collected sayings. Gradually the notion of Sunna expanded to include not only Muhammad's reported words and anecdotes about his deeds, but the actual living practice of a given community of believers. And that growing attitude was in turn based on a Hadith in which Muhammad is reported to have said, "My community will not agree on an error." It followed naturally that the community, striving in good faith to live out the Sunna of the Prophet, embodied a living Sunna that already presupposed an interpretation of Muhammad's example. In simple terms, the community strove to live as Muhammad surely would "if he were here now."

With this expanding notion of Sunna we see the beginnings of a third source of religious law, after Qur'an and Hadith; namely, the consensus or agreed practice of the faithful. Eventually consensus, called *ijma'*, became a technical tool for extending the applicability of the revealed law. If a question arose upon which neither Qur'an nor Hadith made any specific statement, one could seek the solution in the actual practice of the community. The idea is not terribly unlike the classical Roman Catholic notion of *sensus fidelium*, the "conviction of the faithful." It is grass-roots elaboration of how religious persons live out their commitments.

Suppose now that an issue arose upon which neither Qur'an nor Hadith nor actual practice could shed definitive light. What then? In the earliest days of the Islamic expansion, the religious judges *(qadi)* appointed to oversee the ordinary affairs of communities in newly conquered territory were accorded considerable latitude in the exercise of "individual judgment" *(ra'y)*. Many scholars were concerned that the practice was too fluid and easy prey to the unbridled use of personal opinion. As a result, the more informal process of *ra'y* was gradually forged into the more rigorous and tightly controlled tool of reasoning called analogy *(qiyas),* somewhat like what lawyers today call argument from precedent. A rough example might be crack cocaine. Neither Qur'an nor Hadith specifically mention such a thing, and since it has never before surfaced in the local community, one can find no "living Sunna" about the matter. One can then, as a last resort, appeal to analogy. Crack cocaine impairs one's rational faculties. Both Qur'an and Hadith make it clear that intoxicants are forbidden. In addition, the practice of the local community has steadfastly refused to allow such destructive behavior. One can therefore conclude, on the basis of the "link" between an unknown and a known, that revealed law condemns the use of crack cocaine. In sum, Qu'ran, Sunna (as enshrined both in the Hadith and the community's actual practice), consensus and analogical reasoning came to be called the four roots of religious law.

34. Do all Muslims interpret the law in exactly the same way?

Evidence of some variation in legal method dates back to the late seventh century. The community as a whole began elaborating upon various interpretative principles and procedures. Schools of legal methodology came into being, each with its own peculiar emphasis on one or another aspect of juristic thinking. As the initially all-Arab Muslim community came into contact with an ever wider range of ethnic groups and cultures, the need to be able to address new problems grew. Since each culture and ethnic group the Muslims met already had its own legal and religious history, the Muslims had to find ways to put their stamp on the conquered territory without destroying what they found there. They thus had to learn how to incorporate the "customary" law of the place, extending the umbrella of their own system so as to allow the conquered peoples some latitude of practice.

As one might expect, a city like Medina, whose people considered themselves custodians of the original legacy of Muhammad, would naturally tend toward a more cautious and conservative approach. Meanwhile in territories such as Syria and Iraq, frequently—though not always—more innovative and flexible approaches to religious issues were taken.

By the end of the ninth century, about the time the major authoritative written collections of Hadith had come into being, several distinctive schools of jurisprudence had formed. Four Sunni schools remain active today. Each traces its origins back to a founding figure. Abu Hanifa (d. 767) lived and worked in the Iraqi town of Kufa. His school or *madhhab,* the Hanafi or Hanafite, developed a somewhat greater tolerance for the use of analogy than the other schools. Today the Hanafi is the dominant school in Turkey, India, and Pakistan. At the other end of the spectrum stands the school named after Ibn Hanbal (d. 855). A major figure in the religious and intellectual life of ninth-century Baghdad, Ibn Hanbal debated with a group called the Mu'tazilites over their elevation of reason to a position above divine revelation. The harder the Mu'tazilites pushed, the harder Ibn Hanbal pushed back, so that the two sides grew further and further apart. Over the next century or so, the more conservative and traditional approach of Ibn Hanbal became the order of the day. Hanbali influence in our time is limited to the Arabian Peninsula, where it has virtually no competition from other *madhhabs.*

Between the Hanafi and Hanbali schools stand the Shafi'ite, named after Shafi'i (d. c. 819), and the Malikite, founded by Malik ibn Anas (d. 795). The former functions largely in Southeast Asia and parts of Egypt, the latter mostly in North Africa. On the whole, Islamic jurisprudence seeks to strike a balance between individual and community, both in terms of needs, rights, and responsibilities, and in terms of legislative authority. Shi'i legal scholars also developed at least two major law schools, one of which currently dominates the scene in Iran. That school, called the Mujtahidi, emphasizes the requirement for every Muslim to subscribe to the teaching of a particular living *mujtahid,* a legal scholar authorized to exercise independent legal investigation, called *ijtihad.* Whereas, at least in theory, Sunni legal tradition has claimed that the "door of *ijtihad*" swung closed around 900, Shi'i jurisprudence has consistently emphasized the need for ongoing legal elaboration and reinterpretation.

35. Are there any characteristically Muslim views on contemporary social problems, such as poverty and injustice?

In its ideals, Islam has always been a highly service-oriented tradition informed by a keen sense of social responsibility. Among the earliest and most insistent themes in the Qur'an are the call to establish economic justice and to attend to the needs of society's marginalized and disadvantaged. Life in seventh-century Mecca was especially hard for orphans and widows, as well as for the poor. Growth of the local trading economy made it possible for members of privileged clans and families, and even for some individuals, to amass large fortunes at the expense of others. Observing with alarm the growing gap between the haves and the have-nots, Muhammad issued a challenging response in the form of Qur'anic pronouncements and gave further views on matters of social justice in the Hadith. Both sources are full of recommendations that amount to the "works of mercy" that are part of the Christian tradition.

The Qur'an emphasizes a wide range of social responsibilities that run from the simplest ordinary courtesies to what it calls the "steep ascent." But it all begins with proper intention: "Do you see the person in denial of the judgment (to come)? That is the person who drives away the orphan and does not contribute to feeding the poor. Woe betide those who perform their rituals while remaining oblivious to the (meaning of the) prayer; they want only to be seen, but refuse ordinary acts of kindness" (Qur'an 107:1–7). Numerous other texts call on Muslims to "Give to kin, the poor and the traveler what they need; that is best for those who seek the face of God, and they will indeed fare well. What you give in the hope of profiting at the expense of people will gain you nothing in God's sight…" (Qur'an 30:38–39). The "steep ascent" is what the scripture calls the whole demanding project of social responsibility and the difficult task of forming one's conscience accordingly: "What will clarify for you what the steep ascent is? It is freeing a slave, feeding in time of hunger an orphan near of kin, or some poor suffering soul, and being among those who believe and exhort one another to perseverance and encourage each other to compassion" (Qur'an 90:12–17).

Countless hadiths likewise speak of the need for social awareness and action. Muhammad tells of a man who made his living by lending money to others. The man used to say to his assistant, "When you come upon a man who has fallen on hard times, go easy on him, and perhaps God will go easy on us." Muhammad then observed, "And when that employer came to meet God, God went easy on him." All in all, the Muslim tradition issues a demanding call for attention to issues of social morality.

36. Most Christians have heard the term "liberation theology," a movement aimed at lightening the oppression of the poor by applying theological principles to politics. Is there anything like that in Islamic circles?

Beginning in the 1960s a number of Latin American Catholic theologians began articulating a political theology geared to transforming society by enfranchising the poor. In recent times Muslims, too, have sought to devise religiously supported social theories designed to throw off the yoke of oppression that some regard as the legacy of modern colonial domination over much of the Muslim world. Perhaps the most obvious views held by both groups are that theology always has political and social implications and that the poor often suffer at the hands of the privileged members of society. In the view of some Muslim activists, the latter group includes both colonialists and their Muslim collaborators.

Ironically, while Catholics tend to characterize liberation theology as left wing and liberal, those movements among Muslims that are at least roughly parallel are almost always characterized (even by many Muslims) as right wing and reactionary. Muslim thinkers do with the Qur'an and sayings of Muhammad what Catholic liberationists do with their sources: search them for indications of divine sanction for social concern. Naturally there are numerous differences behind these and other apparent similarities, and significant variations among Muslim liberationists as well. But it is important to understand that at least some of the contemporary movements within the Islamic world are motivated by convictions not unlike those of Catholic liberationists.

In fact, there is evidence that in places like India and Southeast Asia Muslim liberationists are very well aware of the work of their Christian counterparts. A major thinker associated with the Iranian revolution, Ali Shariati, has written extensively along these lines. Even some of the Muslim groups that are notorious for their terrorist activities, such as Hamas and the Muslim Brotherhood, have strong and legitimate social-action missions, establishing a range of medical and educational services for the poor. In whatever form, liberation movements are rarely tidy and domestic, calling as they inevitably do for a destabilizing of the status quo. Whether Muslim or Christian, these movements are indeed radical because they foster the rethinking of values and the reordering of society.

Sayyid Qutb (1909–66) of Egypt is a good example of an influential liberation theorist. His thought has become the ideological backbone of the Muslim Brotherhood, founded in 1929 by an Egyptian named Hasan al-Banna (1906–49). Just around the time that Latin American liberation theology was developing, coincidentally, Sayyid Qutb was emerging as a martyr for the cause as a result of his lengthy imprisonment and execution for conspiracy. He argued forcefully on religious grounds for the need to provide educational and economic opportunity for all people.

37. What do Muslims think about birth control and abortion? What about other ethical questions concerning human reproduction, such as in vitro fertilization and surrogate mother- or fatherhood?

Islamic tradition has nearly always considered some form of birth control acceptable under certain specific circumstances. Coitus interruptus, for example, so long as both parties agree to its use, is permissible, especially in view of concerns over anticipated financial problems in caring for a larger family. In more recent times concern over population growth has raised awareness of the need for family planning. But many traditionalist teachers condemn any form of birth control because it invites promiscuity and, when it fails, increases demands for abortion.

On the subject of abortion one finds a wide range of opinions. According to some religious scholars of the Hanafi legal school, abortion is permitted until the fetus is fully formed and ensoulment has occurred (about four months along, according to a Hadith). In the most extreme cases, therapeutic abortions may be allowed after that time in order to protect the mother's life and health, employing the principle that one should choose the lesser of two evils. In such a case established tradition holds that the mother's life takes priority over that of even a fully developed fetus, since the mother has responsibilities and obligations not yet incurred by a fetus. In a case where testing reveals defects in the fetus, a physician may not disclose them or act upon them except insofar as they threaten the mother's life. However, in general the majority opinion seems to be that it is always preferable to bring a child to term, that abortion is unacceptable, and that after four months abortion constitutes murder. At a recent world conference in Cairo, this issue became unexpected common ground uniting Muslims with the representatives from the Vatican. In vitro fertilization with subsequent insertion of the ovum in the biological mother's uterus is considered an acceptable medical solution to a problem such as blockage of the fallopian tubes. On the topic of surrogate motherhood, Islamic law considers the placing of a man's sperm in the womb of a woman other than his wife the equivalent of adultery even if the sperm is placed there by some medical procedure. Minority opinion now allows that medical implantation removes the stigma of adultery, but that the procedure is still unacceptable because of the separation of parental responsibilities and the implications for inheritance legislation. In addition, such an arrangement might also involve sexual abuse of the husband of the woman who has agreed to bear the child, since while his wife is pregnant with someone else's child, her husband's right to conceive with her is denied. Even in a case where a fertilized ovum is inserted in the womb of a surrogate mother, Islamic law considers the woman who actually gives birth to the child its legal mother, eliminating those who contributed the procreative material from any legal claim. In addition, a child thus born is considered illegitimate. In short, Islamic law disallows any version of surrogate parenting and considers all contracts for such agreements invalid. Any attempt to transfer parenthood of a child brought to birth by an outside party is regarded as selling a human being, a serious offense. Two of the problems around surrogacy are the implications for adoption and the child's right to know his or her parentage.

38. Do Muslims have explicit teachings about problems in medical ethics? What do Muslims think about AIDS?

There is no central teaching body or authority for the world's Muslims, and thus no "official" position on these matters to which all are expected to adhere. Nevertheless, contemporary Muslim religious scholars are addressing the difficult medical questions that confront our age. As they address the challenges, these scholars are engaging in the Islamic analogy to Christian "moral theology" or "theological ethics," attempting to interpret the sources of the tradition in light of contemporary experience—and vice versa. And the practical outcome is religious law.

Muslim religious law recognizes a spectrum of five categories used to characterize human acts. At opposite ends of the spectrum are acts considered either "required" or "forbidden"; squarely in the middle are those considered moral and legally neutral; and to either side of those indifferent acts are those labeled either "recommended" or "disapproved." Not all religious scholars will necessarily arrive at the same conclusion as to the categories in which all questionable acts belong, since both Sunni and Shiʻi Muslims recognize several variations in legal methodology. What is important here is that moral decisions are highly nuanced. Still more important is the fundamental notion that the human body is not merely a highly sophisticated machine that functions according to a set of mechanical and chemical laws, but a vessel of the spirit that has its own needs in addition to its spiritual function. The prime ethical responsibility of both the individual person and those involved in health care is to base all decisions on an assessment that balances both the rights accorded a human body in Islamic law (rights to food and shelter, for example) and the ultimate purpose of the body. The overriding principle is the sanctity of life as a gift from the sovereign Creator, in whose merciful care every human destiny abides.

In some regional populations in central Africa with heavy concentrations of Muslims, the incidence of AIDS has been tragically high, but Muslims everywhere are and will continue to be affected by the AIDS crisis. Like their non-Muslim brothers and sisters, Muslims too have continually to summon up reserves of compassion and to struggle against the temptation to be judgmental toward persons with AIDS. Like some Christians, some Muslims are inclined to interpret the incidence of the disease as divine punishment for immoral behavior. But since it is clear that AIDS does not respect many boundaries, Muslims face the challenge of helping to turn the tide of a major threat to the societies in which they live, wherever they may be. The majority opinion among religiously engaged Muslims is simply this: sexual promiscuity and the use of illegal drugs, the kinds of voluntary behavior often responsible for the spread of AIDS, are unacceptable, and Muslims have a duty to counsel against them. People who are aware that individuals they know have engaged in high-risk activities have a responsibility to recommend screening. In short, the majority

Muslim view concerning AIDS calls for compassion, understanding, and prayer along with active social concern wherever that is clearly warranted.

39. What basic views do Muslims hold on human rights?

Closely related to the Islamic concern for economic justice is the desire not to let the rights of the individual become swallowed up by those of society as a whole. It seeks a balance between the rampant individualism many Muslims associate with capitalist cultures, and the stifling of individual initiative frequently identified with totalitarian systems. Many Muslims think of Islam as the last bastion of genuine egalitarianism under God. Like all the rest of us, they have had a hard time translating ideals into realities.

Muslims trace the origin of "human rights" issues in their tradition back to Muhammad. Two early documents form the basic charter. Shortly after the Hijra, Muhammad promulgated what came to be known as the "Constitution of Medina," in which he set out the principal terms governing the relationships of Muslims to one another and to the non-Muslim groups in the region. Equally fundamental are several of the stipulations of Muhammad's "Farewell Sermon," delivered in 632 C.E., during his final pilgrimage to Mecca. That document contains basic statements about important social relationships. This sample gives a sense of its tone: "Your lives and property are sacred and inviolable among one another...[You] have rights over your wives and your wives have rights over you. Treat your wives with kindness and love....The aristocracy of old is trampled under my feet. The Arab has no superiority over the non-Arab and the non-Arab has no superiority over the Arab. All are children of Adam and Adam was made of earth....Know that all Muslims are brothers unto one another. You are one brotherhood. Nothing that belongs to another is lawful to his brother, unless freely given. Guard yourselves against committing injustice...."

Muslim writers often situate human rights within the context of "God's Rights." God has the right to, but no need of, human beings' faith, acceptance of divine guidance, obedience, and worship. The Qur'an makes the very direct statement that "There is no compulsion in religion" (Qur'an 2:256). Many Muslims take that to mean that all persons are free to respond to God's signs as they please. Islamic history is full of examples of what Marshal Hodgson calls the triumph of the universalistic spirit, in which Muslims and non-Muslims lived together in harmony. At times, however, the spirit of "partisanship" has dominated, with disastrous consequences.

Various modern reforms have seen dramatic change in a number of nations with strong Muslim majorities, usually in connection with developments in constitutional forms of government. But there have generally been trade-offs. For example, the modern Turkish republic superseded the Ottoman Empire in the 1920s and proclaimed a range of human rights unsupported previously; but the republic also suppressed the religious freedom of Muslims who posed a threat to its secularizing program. The Iranian revolutionary constitution also proclaimed its support of economic, social, and cultural rights, but put severe limits on political and civil rights.

A "Universal Islamic Declaration of Human Rights," promulgated in 1981 by an Islamic Council, a nonauthoritative body made up of invited members from a number of Middle Eastern and south Asian Muslim countries, represents one of the fullest recent articulations of Islamic values on the subject. The document affirms a "commitment to uphold the following inviolable and inalienable human rights that we consider are enjoined by Islam"—right to life, freedom, equality, justice, fair trial, protection against abuse of power, torture, protection of reputation, asylum, minority protection, participation in public affairs, freedom of belief, freedom of thought and speech, freedom of religion, free association, economic order, protection of property, worker dignity, social security, family integrity, protection of rights of married women, education, privacy, freedom of movement, and freedom of residence. In 1990 the Organization of the Islamic Conference, whose membership includes representatives of virtually all the nations with majority Muslim populations, put forth a charter of rights, but it differs from the International Bill of Human Rights advanced by the United Nations in that the Islamic charter continues to subsume all rights under the controlling authority of religious law, or *shari'a*.

40. I'm sure it's important for Muslims to trace all key values back to the Qur'an and Muhammad; but what about putting these values into action?

Concerned Muslims in our time have focused considerable attention on questions of human rights. As is the case with human rights organizations all over the world, those that have formed within the greater Islamic community often have lacked the political clout needed to bring about effective change in governmental policy. Evidence of violations apparently sanctioned at the highest levels in certain nations whose populations are predominantly Muslim, has prompted some outside observers to criticize Muslims for failing to safeguard basic human rights. The charge is misdirected. Critics would argue that where Muslims are "in control," and preach the unity of religious and civil spheres, they have no excuse for not implementing Islam's loftiest values in their societies. Such criticism fails to take note of a pair of unpleasant realities. First, when ostensibly religious ideals are explicitly incorporated into political programs, they often get pushed aside by more pressing pragmatic concerns, even as government spokespersons continue to employ religious rhetoric. In short, Muslims, like the rest of us, don't always live up to their stated ideals. Second, religious ideals that are so appropriated are often quite selective, do not represent the tradition's full scope, and thus fail to take account of conflicting claims.

Islamic ideals in this respect are extremely high and, like all such challenging aspirations, are very difficult to put into practice. One can cite numerous contemporary examples of Muslim efforts to articulate principles of human rights. Some years ago, Pakistan hosted an International Islamic Seminar on the Application of the Revealed Law. In a statement obviously meant to refute a number of charges, the Seminar declared: "...the Islamic code of life lays down not only moral, but social, economic, political, cultural and educational norms and rules based on the principles of equality, brotherhood and justice...the Islamic code is designed to create a just and free society in which every individual enjoys equal rights and equal opportunities regardless of rank, birth, caste, color, or creed." Political traditions in many countries nevertheless often stand between the formulation of ideals and their implementation.

FIVE:

SPIRITUALITY

41. "Spirituality" is a widely and often loosely used term; could you define what you mean by it relation to Islam?

By the term "spirituality" I mean the various ways a religious tradition describes and facilitates the unfolding experience of a relationship between individual believers, as members of a faith community, and the source and goal of the individual's existence. Emphasizing the experiential and relational aspects of religion, the study of spirituality focuses on how the tradition assists its members to discover and cultivate their inmost selves, and to embark on a lifelong journey toward their ultimate end. Unlike the study of theology, that of spirituality allows one to take fuller account of affective and devotional themes, while deemphasizing doctrinal and other more technical matters.

Islamic spirituality includes a wide range of issues. Beginning, as always, with the Qur'an and traditions of Muhammad, Muslims have developed ways of reading and interpreting the sacred sources with an eye for references to God's nearness. In addition, Muslim writers, poets, and artists across the world have evolved dozens of literary and visual forms by which to express their experience of God's presence in everything from communal ritual prayer to glorying in a sunset to the tragedy of heartbreaking loss. Muslims can draw upon a rich repository of spiritual models as well, stories of men and women whose achievements mark them as especially favored by God. Through books, pictures, and performance, their example continues to inspire, challenge, and entertain Muslims in search of greater depth to their faith.

Since an integral part of Muslim identity is the sense of belonging to a society of believers, the study of Islamic spirituality has also to take into account the various ways Muslims have fostered community through their development of institutions such as mosques, schools, hospitals, and religious confraternities. Beyond the kind of basic religious education that Muslims have traditionally passed along to their children, spiritual theologians and other specialists have also developed sophisticated principles and finely tuned techniques both for assisting seekers toward more advanced progress along the spiritual path, and for analyzing that progress. Finally, perhaps the most difficult and subtle materials are the records of personal experience—autobiographies, diaries, and ecstatic utterances—left by some of Islam's most colorful and enigmatic mystical characters.

42. One often hears Muslims characterized as "ritualistic." Can you clarify that?

People who are seriously engaged in their own religious traditions frequently regard the religious practices of others as mechanical and rote. Every tradition—even the so-called nonliturgical ones—has its rituals, but some are more elaborate than others. Other people's rituals inevitably strike outsiders as strange, simply because religious ritual is among the more obvious features that distinguish insiders from outsiders. And religious ritual is highly vulnerable to caricature: Catholics are the ones who watch a priest go through a bunch of strange motions and say strange words; Muslims are the ones who bob up and down facing Mecca; Hindus are the ones who offer food to statues with lots of arms….Many people have a hard time demystifying the actions they associate with the religious practice of others, but it is important to keep in mind that there is a reason for all of it, and that ritual endures because it works in some important way.

Any ritual can become a matter of habit, just a question of going through the motions. Muslims are no more likely than non-Muslims to take the deeper meaning of their rituals for granted. In fact, Islamic tradition deals with the problem very directly, teaching that a deliberate awareness of intention *(niyya)* must precede the performance of every act of worship. Apart from right intention, deeds of piety have no religious meaning. At a still deeper level, one needs the enduring habit of "presence of the heart" in order to approach each individual act of devotion with the mental and spiritual focus required to articulate the intention.

A good example of this is the requirement of ritual purification prior to performing the ritual prayer. Ordinarily, worshipers have access to water with which to cleanse face, hands, arms, and feet. But, if at prayer time water is not available to a traveler, for example, he or she may use sand or even dust. This alternative provision suggests a nonliteral understanding of purification as a change of mind and heart. In addition, the term *masjid,* usually translated as "mosque," means "place of prostration," and that can be any place so designated by a deliberate appropriation of the space for spiritual purposes. Intention and purification prepare the worshiper to move temporarily into another way of being by stepping out of the ordinary rhythms of daily life into sacred time and space. For attentive Muslims, the five daily moments of ritual prayer become a way of sanctifying time. The orientation toward Mecca, whether one is praying in the mosque or elsewhere, with or without a prayer rug, is a way of sanctifying place, creating a sacred space. Ultimately it is not the external action that counts, but the quality of the relationship between worshiper and Worshiped that the action expresses.

43. Do Muslims engage in other forms of prayer besides the *salat?*

In addition to the practice of the five daily ritual prayers, offered in concert with millions of others, the Islamic tradition recommends a variety of private devotional or "free" prayer, usually called by the generic term *du'a,* or supplication. The best prayer is any that Muhammad first pronounced. Even the angels took their cue from the Prophet. A favorite prayer of Muhammad's was one that he recommended Muslims pray on their pilgrim way to Mecca: "O God, indeed you know and see where I stand and hear what I say. You know me inside and out; nothing of me is hidden from you. And I am the lowly, needy one who seeks your aid and sanctuary, aware of my sinfulness in shame and confusion. I make my request of you as one who is poor; as a humbled sinner I make my plea; fearful in my blindness I call out to you, head bowed before you, eyes pouring out tears to you, body grown thin for you, face in the dust at your feet. O God, as I cry out to you, do not disappoint me; but be kind and compassionate to me, you who are beyond any that can be petitioned, most generous of any that give, most merciful of those who show mercy [a reference to Qur'an 12]. Praise to God, Lord of the universe."

Sometimes one cannot find the appropriate words for prayer; perhaps no words at all come trippingly to the tongue. In moments like these, heart's desire and mind's intent more than make up for whatever else seems lacking. The thirteenth-century mystical poet Rumi tells a marvelous tale about a pious Muslim who made haste one Friday toward

the mosque. Muhammad was leading the community in the congregational prayer that day, and the man was particularly eager to be there
with them. Arriving at the mosque, he found a crowd emerging and
asked why they were leaving early. They replied that he was simply too
late, for Muhammad had just dismissed them with a blessing. At that the
man heaved such a sigh of frustrated longing that his heart smoked
("sigh" is "heart smoke" in Persian). One of those just leaving the
mosque noticed the sigh and was so taken by it that he said "I will trade
you all of my formal prayer for that one sigh of yours." The latecomer
agreed to the swap. Later that evening, as the man who accepted the
sigh went off to sleep, a voice assured him, "You have bought the water
of life and healing. To honor your choice, I accept the ritual prayer of all
my people."

Rumi tells another story about a man who prayed devoutly, keeping vigil late into the night. Once when he began to tire and weaken in
his resolve to persevere, Satan saw his chance and planted a suggestion
in his weary soul. For all your calling out "O God," have you ever once
heard God reply "Here I am"? The man had to admit he had never
detected even a faint whisper in reply. God took note of all this and sent
a messenger to the praying man. All of the fear and love the man had
poured into his invocation, the messenger assured him, were already
God's gift, unrequested and unrealized. "Beneath every 'O Lord' of
yours lies many a 'Here I am' from me." No one seeks God but that God
has first planted the desire to seek; the answer is prior to the question.

In prayer as in so many other dimensions of the spiritual life,
Abraham sets the example. Rumi notes that where there is no sighing,
there is no ecstasy; and Abraham was the "sighful man" par excellence.
When the patriarch prayed, his personal commitment and intensity
caused his heart to bubble. You could hear Abraham praying for miles.

44. Could you give a few more examples of that kind of prayer?

Muhammad himself left a number of prayers that have remained
popular, such as this request, reminiscent of the Lord's Prayer, that God
heal a sick member of his community: "God our Lord, you who are in
the heavens, may your name be sanctified. Yours is the command in the
heavens and on earth. As your mercy is in the heavens, so let your

mercy be on earth. Forgive our sins and failures. You are the Lord of those who seek to do good. Upon this illness send down mercy from your mercy and healing from your healing." Here is a prayer Muhammad is said to have prayed for himself: "O God, guide me among those you have guided, and sustain me among those you have sustained. Make me your intimate friend among those you have made your intimate friends. Bless me in what you have given me." And this gem of simplicity and directness: "O God, create light in my heart, and light in my eye, and light in my hearing, and light on my right, and light on my left, light above me, light below me, light in front of me, light behind me. Create light for me: on my tongue, light; in my muscles, light; in my flesh, light; in my hair, light; in my body, light; in my soul, light. Make light grow for me. O God, grant me light!"

Some of the most vivid and evocative prayers have come from the great mystics, such as Junayd (d. 910) of Baghdad. He addresses God: "I have come to realize that you are in my inmost being, and I have conversed with you intimately. We are in a way, then, united, but in a way we are quite separated. Even if your sublime grandeur has kept you inaccessible to my eye's glance, still, loving ecstasy has caused me to feel your touch within me."

The martyr-mystic al-Hallaj (d. 922) describes his awareness of God as he reads the "signs within the self." "O God, the sun neither rises nor sets but that your love is one with my breathing. Never have I sat in conversation, but that it was you who spoke to me from among those seated round. Never have I been mindful of you, either in sadness or rejoicing, but that you were there in my heart amidst my inmost whisperings. Never have I decided on a drink of water in my thirst, but that I saw your image in the cup." Elsewhere Hallaj says God is so close as to "flow between my heart and its sheath as tears flow between eye and eyelid."

A number of Islam's women mystics, too, have left us samples of their favorite prayers. After the night ritual prayer was over, Rabi'a al-Adawiya (d. 801) liked to pray: "Eyes are heavy with sleep, unaware of their forgetfulness. And still Rabi'a the sinner abides in your presence in the hope that you might look on her with a gaze that will keep sleep from diminishing her service of you. By your power and majesty, may I not slacken in serving you either night or day until I meet you (in death)." A younger contemporary named Zahra prayed: "You whose powers are without limit, you the munificent and eternal, make the eyes of my heart rejoice in the gardens of your power. Join my anxious care to your tender largesse, O gracious one. In your majesty and splendor take me away from the paths of those who only make a show of power, O compassionate one. Make me a servant and a seeker, and be, O light of my heart and ultimate desire, my Friend."

45. Does Muhammad play a role in Islamic spirituality anything like that of Jesus in Christian spirituality? And what about saints—do they have a place?

Since Muslims regard Muhammad as no more than a human being, while Christians believe Jesus is divine, the two figures naturally occupy very different positions in the spiritualities of their respective traditions. That is not to suggest, however, that Muhammad occupies a *lesser* place for Muslims—just different from a theological perspective. Muhammad's first role is that of a teacher and model. In addition to serving as the foremost conduit of revelation, the Prophet is the prime exemplar for virtually every facet of the life of piety and virtue. He models spiritual values of fatherly and spousal devotion, of justice and fairness, and of responsible and selfless leadership. The other prophets share some of Muhammad's limelight in this respect, since they too brought revelation and were, collectively, humanity's proudest boast.

Muhammad has also functioned for many Muslims as a focus of intense popular devotion. As the creature who enjoys the most intimate relationship with God, Muhammad elicits extraordinary outpourings of affection from Muslims the world over. Even in countries that officially consider festivities in honor of the Prophet's birthday as extravagant or theologically unwarranted, devout Muslims invariably express their feelings for Muhammad quite effusively. Many people implore Muhammad's intercession with God for the fulfillment of a variety of needs. Some even ask the Prophet directly to bestow on them his spiritual power and blessing *(baraka)*.

Muslim mystics have often interpreted Muhammad as the model for their spiritual quest, especially in his experience of the Night Journey and Ascension. Some Sufis have considered Muhammad as the ultimate shaykh, the celestial spiritual guide who appears in dreams to initiate individuals into the Sufi Order by conferring upon them the symbolic patched frock. The more speculative mystics have even pictured Muhammad as a cosmic being, the Perfect Person whose spiritual presence suffuses all of creation. At this end of the theological spectrum, which majority theological opinion generally regards as at least innovation if not outright heresy, Muhammad bears some similarity to the cosmic Christ of the New Testament Letter to the Ephesians.

Finally, Muslim tradition recognizes a number of paradigmatic figures called Friends of God, who play a role in Islamic spirituality roughly analogous to that of Christianity's saints. Friends of God are considered distinct from prophets, even though both are capable of manifesting God's power in miraculous deeds. Miracles granted through prophets are known as evidentiary miracles *(mu'jizat),* effected to establish the veracity of the prophet's claim, whereas saintly miracles are called "wonders" *(karamat).* Friends of God are very important in popular piety, though in many places Muslim authorities are mounting massive education campaigns to purge Islam of the vestiges of what they consider un Islamic superstition.

46. Is forgiveness an important theme in Islamic spirituality? Do Muslims have anything analogous to the Catholic sacrament of reconciliation?

Along with the divine names "Compassionate" *(rahman)* and "Merciful" *(rahim),* the names "Forgiver" *(ghafur),* "Forgiving" *(ghaffar),* "Oft-turning" or "Relenting" *(tawwab),* and "Pardoning" *(afuw)* are among the most used in prayer and frequently discussed by Muslim spiritual writers. A Sacred Hadith says that God descends to the lowest heaven during the third watch of each night and calls out, "Is there anyone who seeks my forgiveness, that I might forgive?" According to a Hadith, Muhammad said, "My heart is clouded until I have sought God's forgiveness seventy times day and night." Dozens of other sayings like these about both God and Muhammad appear in large sections of the great collections of Hadith dedicated to traditions about forgiveness and repentance. The term for "seeking forgiveness" from God *(istighfar)* has the root meaning of asking that God "cover over" or "render ineffective" one's evil actions. The term for repentance *(tawba)* means "turning around." Islamic sources convey a vivid sense of God's infinite patience and of the need for human beings to learn, after the example of Muhammad, to embody forbearance in their daily lives.

Ideally, one's repentance arises not out of fear of a God who will exact vengeance of the sinner, a divine despot who wields the threat of eternal damnation. Fear of hell might help "jump-start" individuals who are particularly heedless, but in the long run the desired motive is the simple conviction that, as the Muslim saying goes, "God's mercy outweighs his wrath." Awareness of God's tender mercies is also a natural corrective for scrupulosity, for God taxes no soul beyond its limit and requires only that each person sincerely seek to rid his or her life of false gods, whatever shape they may take.

Forgiveness is as important in human relations as in the individual's relationship with God. The Qur'an teaches often that one should dispense with grudges as soon as possible, insisting that even in divorce the separating partners must seek to forgive each other (2:237). Those who refuse to forgive and be reconciled with others can hardly expect that God will deal gently with them in the final accounting. A saying of Muhammad sums it all up: "If anyone continually asks pardon, God will show that person a way out of every difficulty and respite from every anxiety, with sustenance from where he least expected it."

47. Is the Qur'an as important in Islamic spirituality as the Bible is in Christian spirituality?

In some ways it is even more prominent in the spiritual practice of many Muslims. The Qur'an forms the core of all Islamic worship and devotional activity. As part of the daily ritual prayer, Muslims regularly recite the opening sura quoted earlier, as well as several other short pieces. An example is the very brief Sura 112, *al-Ikhlas* (Sincerity or Purity of Faith): "Proclaim: He is One God, God the besought of all; He does not beget; He is not begotten; and there is none like Him." It unmistakably reminds Muslims that they are different from Christians who believe in Father, Son, and Spirit. But perhaps just as important as the theological content is the sheer physical experience of reciting and/or hearing recitation of the Qur'an. The effect on listeners is often profound, for the mode of delivery combined with the extraordinarily earthy sound of Arabic make for an intensely moving experience. One commentator has likened the recitation to the Christian practice of communion, in that in both instances, one has the Word on the tongue.

Qur'an recitation is also part of many religious occasions outside the five daily prayers. After a funeral, families of the deceased often hire a reciter to come and grace the time for condolence with appropriate scriptural texts. During the fasting month of Ramadan, Muslims make a special place for recitation. They commemorate the 27th of that lunar month as the "Night of Power," when Muhammad received the first revelation. In addition, the entire Qur'an is recited during the thirty nights of Ramadan. For that and other such "liturgical" purposes, the text of the scripture has been divided into thirty sections, each of which is further halved, and those halves further quartered, yielding a total of 240 divisions. One can easily keep track of how far one has to go during each period of recitation.

There are further social dimensions as well. All across the Islamic world, the art of Qur'an recitation is highly prized. One can almost always tune to a radio station that broadcasts recitation and commentary all day. In some places, such as Malaysia and Indonesia and even on a smaller scale here in the United States, the art has become very competitive. National contests draw huge crowds to sports stadiums, and winners look forward to going to a grand final competition in Mecca. And in virtually any large Cairene mosque, for example, one can find people sitting alone and chanting their recitation quietly to themselves, or engaged in lively discussions about the text.

On the level of individual devotion as well, the Qur'an functions prominently. Some Muslims still strive to memorize the entire book, approximately six thousand verses. Memorizing the text means having it in one's heart and "keeping" it there. Paralleling the memorization of the Qur'an is what has been called the Qur'anization of the memory. The phrase originally referred to the intensely scriptural way of thinking manifested by some of the great Muslim spiritual writers and mystical poets. But there are further implications as well. Especially throughout the Arabic speaking world, phrases from the Qur'an have become so much a part of ordinary speech, particularly among very tradition-minded Muslims, that many people no longer know where the sacred ends and the profane begins.

48. Is there such a thing as Islamic asceticism?

At the core of Islamic spirituality is the concept of life as constant striving or struggle *(jihad)*. Jihad has carried from the earliest days a variety of meanings other than that associated with the use of violence. According to a Hadith, a young man told Muhammad how desperately he wanted to join his fellow Muslims in defending the faith. Muhammad asked whether the young man's parents were growing old. When he said they were, the Prophet told the youth to consider taking care of them as his jihad. Jihad includes even the smallest and apparently least significant action, so long as it represents genuine effort, every struggle and sacrifice made "in the way of God." Thus, expressing the truth, exhorting others to act justly, discouraging injustice, and sacrificing one's own resources and even one's life, if necessary, are part of meritorious struggle. Muslim tradition speaks of jihad of the pen, of the tongue, of the mind, as well as of the sword. Above all, jihad means personal and communal discipline.

Islamic tradition does not sanctify self-denial as a way of life. All of the good things God gives are to be enjoyed to the full as reminders of the divine generosity. Self-denial does have its place, however. The fast of Ramadan, the provision of alms, and attention to daily ritual prayer are all very demanding practices, but they are means rather than ends in themselves. Their ultimate purpose is to help believers keep things in perspective: every good thing comes from God and returns to God. Spiritual practice is meant to keep that reality ever before the believer.

Life's ordinary difficulties are God's way of testing and strengthening people, a form of ongoing discipline. There have, of course, been various ascetical movements of a more pronounced type from time to time during Islamic history. And the history of Sufism in particular evidences several remarkable examples of the institutionalization of ascetical practice, but they represent a small portion of Islamic society at any given time. A text from the Qur'an sums up a number of the central themes in Islamic spirituality and relates them, in the last verse, to this question of spiritual discipline: "Uprightness is not a question of turning your faces to the *qibla* of East or West. Uprightness means rather believing in God and in the final day, and in the angels and the Book and the prophets. It means sharing your wealth, dear as it is to you (some translate this phrase "out of love for Him"), with kinfolk, orphans, the poor, the traveler (literally "son of the road"), those who come asking, and for setting slaves free. It means performing the ritual prayer *(salat),* giving alms *(zakat),* living up to one's solemn word, and bearing up under the most intense hardship and in dire straits" (Qur'an 2:177).

49. How did Islamic mysticism develop? What is the meaning of the term "Sufism"?

Islam does indeed have an extraordinarily rich tradition of mysticism, and Sufism has become the term most commonly used to refer to Islamic mysticism. By way of background, it will be helpful to sketch the development of the principal institutions associated with Sufism. Very early in Islamic history, individuals in such diverse cities as Medina, Damascus, and Baghdad became known for expressions of their personal piety. Detractors, of course, considered them eccentric, or felt they were going against a Hadith that seemed to rule out monklike practices (though there are other Hadiths in which Muhammad is reported to speak highly of certain forms of asceticism.)

Out of the early ascetical movement, which arose partly as a protest against the increasingly regal style of the Umayyad caliphs, grew the beginnings of mysticism. Around the end of the eighth century in Baghdad a woman named Rabi'a appeared who became the first great mystical poet who dared speak of her loving relationship with God. Within a century, more such poets appeared, speakers of Persian as well as of Arabic, all over the central Middle East. Gradually, small groups of seekers began to cluster around these and other holy persons. Such informal circles were the beginnings of what would later develop into formally constituted religious orders, the first of which appeared in the twelfth century under the famous and still widely popular shaykh Abd al-Qadir al-Jilani (d. 1166). The term *tariqa* or "personal spiritual path," originally used to describe the individual's search for God, came to refer to the formal orders. Each seeker thus became an aspirant, an initiate, and an adept within a particular Tariqa. As in the Christian tradition, many of the orders grew and spread rapidly, some splitting into suborders and establishing their own variant of the original founder's charism.

Groups at first small enough to meet and even take shelter in the homes of the shaykhs and shaykhas (female spiritual guides) eventually outgrew those accommodations. Thus were founded the first Sufi architectural designs intended to provide for all of the formal and functional needs of the orders—residential, ritual, and social, including libraries and soup kitchens. These are called variously *zawiya, khanqa,* or *tekkiye.* Many such foundations eventually included a funerary facility, beginning as the burial places of founders and later serving as cemeteries for subsequent shaykhs and administrators of the orders.

Within that institutional framework, the Sufi mystical tradition developed a number of spiritual disciplines and exercises designed to aid the traveler in keeping to the Path. As Muhammad needed the guidance of Gabriel on his passage to the Unseen World, so everyone requires assistance in reading the signs within the self.

Surviving along with a number of formerly more highly visible religious orders is the gathering of seekers for a prayer service (known as *dhikr*) that often involves ritual recitation of the Qur'an, chanting of mantralike words and phrases in Arabic, and dancing. In Cairo, for example, during festivities honoring holy persons such as members of the Prophet's family, one can find groups of people engaging in ritual dancing and chanting.

50. I've heard that there are Sufis in this country who get together to sing and dance as part of a religious ceremony. Some say they're Muslims and some say it doesn't make any difference what your religion is; anybody can be a Sufi. Who's correct?

Sufism, the usual translation of the Arabic term *tasawwuf,* has been variously interpreted throughout its history. Some Sufi groups in the U.S. clearly understand themselves as Muslims and are careful to observe mainstream Islamic practices and religious law. Some so-called Sufi groups have become totally disconnected with Islam and define Sufism as a vaguely, but not necessarily, religious form of mysticism and ecstatic behavior that transcends all confessional boundaries. This kind of interpretation seems to arise from statements made by some of the greatest Sufi poets, some of whom raised more than a few eyebrows in their own time. However, when mystical poets such as Jalal ad-Din

Rumi (d. 1274) and Fakhr ad-Din Iraqi (d. 1289) and others made statements apparently suggesting that true belief and love of God transport
one beyond the boundaries of traditional communities of faith, they did
not intend for their listeners and readers to take them literally. They
were not rejecting Islam, but rather attempting to express the paradox of
any authentic personal relationship to God. God, they reasoned, is bigger than all of our petty divisions—including those our religious boundaries seem to create. In that sense no religious community is big enough
to express the fullness of God, but the great Sufi teachers have never
dispensed with the need for active participation in the life of the community of Muslims.

51. How do Muslims deal with death and bereavement?

Before a burial, mourners gather in a mosque, or in front of the
deceased person's house, or in a specially constructed enclosure, to pronounce the *takbir* ("God is Supreme," *Allahu akbar*) four times.
Although the *takbir* is part of all Muslim prayer and begins the call to
prayer itself, its prominence in the funeral rite is such that saying the
takbir is equivalent to saying, "this person (or thing in other contexts) is
dead to me," that is, I have surrendered this to God. All attention falls on
God's grandeur so that nothing else can distract.

Loneliness is among the most feared sufferings of the tomb.
Prayers popular throughout the Islamic world make this very evident.
The idea that the spirit returns to the body in the grave heightens the
apprehension that the deceased will experience a terrible solitude and
acute pain of separation. A final graveside prayer from Egypt says: "O
God, Companion of every lonely one, Present One who are never a
stranger, Near One when others are far, be the Companion O God of our
loneliness and his (the deceased) loneliness, have mercy on our strangeness and his strangeness, and whiten his page [i.e., forgive sin] and forgive us and forgive him and forgive the one who stood over his grave to
say: 'There is no god but God, and Muhammad is the Messenger of
God.'" Many believe that after the burial they may apply the merit of
their prayers toward the mitigation of the grave's terrors.

Shortly after Muhammad's death, his successor, Abu Bakr, is
reported to have addressed the crowd keeping vigil outside the house in

Medina: "If you worship Muhammad, know that he is dead; if you worship God, know that he lives forever." According to conflicting Hadiths, Muhammad both encouraged and forbade Muslims to visit his tomb. Most pilgrims to Mecca opt for the positive tradition and go to pray at the Prophet's grave. A popular belief that salvation is assured to anyone who dies at or en route to the pilgrimage goal is no doubt enhanced by the inclusion of Muhammad's tomb among the customary sites of the pilgrim's circuit.

Most Muslims will die without having the opportunity to visit Muhammad's grave, but few will lack the blessing of a symbolic presence of the Prophet at theirs. The following prayer that Muhammad is said to have offered at the funerals of early Muslims is still in use, as are many others like it: "O God, forgive the living among us and those of us who have died; those present and those absent; the small and the great among us; our women and our men. O God, make alive with grateful surrender *[islam]* whomever among us you cause to remain alive; and cause to die in the faith whichever of us you cause to die. O God, do not keep from us the reward awaiting the deceased, and do not make life hard for us with this passing."

In many parts of the Islamic world the fifteenth day of the eighth lunar month, Sha'ban, calls for special reflection on human mortality and the remembrance of the dead. According to tradition, the tree of life is shaken on the eve of that day. On the leaves are written the names of the living, and all whose leaves fall in the shaking will die during the next year. Of course, no one alive knows whose leaves have fallen; so many people take the occasion to offer prayers like this Shi'ite petition: "Have mercy on me on the day when I come before you alone, my gaze turned towards you, my deeds tied round my neck, all creatures dissociating themselves from me, yes even my father and my mother and those for whom I toiled and strove. Then if you do not show me mercy who will have mercy upon me?…Who will teach my tongue to speak when I am alone with my deeds, and am asked concerning those things that you know better than I?"

Surely the single most important communal observance of death and its ultimate significance occurs in the Shi'ite commemoration of the martyrdom of Husayn, who died at the Iraqi site of Karbala in 680 while confronting the evil caliph Yazid. Beginning on the first day of the first lunar month, Muharram, Shi'ites participate vicariously in Husayn's redemptive suffering and death. A ten-day observance includes various penances, self-flagellation, processions of mourning, and culminates (at least in more traditional areas) in the "passion play" of Karbala. Scenes in the elaborate drama vary with locality, but always include aspects of the paradigmatic sufferings of earlier prophets such as Abraham, Noah, and Moses. In the finale the actors play out Husayn's tragic death; grandfather Muhammad persuades Husayn not only to forgive, but to intercede on behalf of his murderers. Sunni Muslims place far less significance on Husayn's death, but veneration of saints and small pilgrimages *(ziyara)* to their tombs are still common in many places.

Six:

Cultural and Intellectual Themes

52. Some say that Muslims and Christians have such a hard time understanding each other because the Islamic world never experienced either a "Renaissance" or an "Enlightenment." Is that true?

Let me begin with a classic Islamic story. Once upon a time an itinerant grammarian came to a body of water and enlisted the services of a boatman to ferry him across. Attempting to strike up a conversation on his favorite topic, the grammarian asked the boatman, "Do you know the science of grammar?" The humble boatman thought for a moment and responded rather disappointedly that he did not. A while later a gathering storm threatened to capsize the small vessel. Said the boatman to the grammarian, "Do you know the science of swimming?"

Both men had their abilities, their special interests; but they had a hard time meeting because each one was looking at life through very different lenses and beginning from very different assumptions about what is most important. A key question here is: enlightened compared to what? Point of view depends a great deal on what one regards as critical at any given moment in history. Many European and American non-Muslims have gotten into the habit of looking at the world through the filters of Renaissance and Enlightenment values. The view has become so accepted that some are convinced that any other view must be either naive or just plain wrong. Viewed from that perspective, Islam appears to some as the last holdout against a Renaissance appreciation of the centrality of humanistic values and the Enlightenment's critical intelligence. Islam thus represents for some a refusal to view the world rationally and critically. For many Muslims, on the other hand, the Renaissance is virtually synonymous with presumptuous anthropocentrism, and the Enlightenment with the arrogant denial of the ultimately divine causality of all events.

A major symbolic issue for many Muslims is the pervasive feeling that the tendency of Euro-American non-Muslims to apply the Renaissance-Enlightenment yardstick to Islamic history and culture and find it wanting is just another example of "western" cultural imperialism. They resent the implication that Muslims are somehow genetically medieval and need to be "fixed" by an injection of critical thinking. The more outsiders insist that Muslims need to shed traditional notions such as the classical ideal of the unity of civil and religious spheres, the more Muslims ask why. Revolutionary changes in worldview, what some have called paradigm shifts, have indeed been afoot among Muslims of our time. As is always the case with dramatic change, however, wide acceptance happens very gradually: neither the Renaissance nor the Enlightenment caught on overnight.

53. But aren't there still some fundamental differences between the ways that the two traditions approach the relationships between faith and reason, or between revelation and science?

Both Christianity and Islam have long histories of wrestling with their relationships to culture and learning. Many Christians oddly enough seem to have been taken in by the stereotyped notion that Islam is anti-intellectual, while many Muslims have seen Christians as easy prey to secularism. Neither view takes account of the actual role of culture in the history of either tradition. It is a complex matter. Islam's tradition of highly developed cultural and educational strengths goes back to the Prophet's reputation for concern with learning. He counseled Muslims to seek knowledge even as far as China; called the scholar's ink holier than the blood of martyrs; and observed that a single scholar is harder on Satan than a thousand ascetics. (Another saying, however, notes that a handful of luck is sometimes more useful than six camel loads of books!)

Likewise, the notion entertained by many Muslims that "the West" is somehow inherently opposed to religion in general and to Islam in particular misses the point. Wherever Muslims live, whether in Pakistan or the Middle East or Indonesia or the United States of America, they must make some sort of accommodation to cultural forces. Christians can feel a great deal of sympathy with the words of the Hadith, "Islam came into the world a stranger and will go out a stranger." In this country, at least, Muslims and Christians have a great deal to say to each other about maintaining their values in the face of enormous cultural pressures to the contrary. The ultimate Renaissance/humanistic contribution to Muslim-

Christian relations would be perhaps a greater understanding of our mutual xenophobias. Why do we have such terrible difficulty accepting otherness? Both traditions possess the tools for critical assessment of culture, and they need to be shared. Both Muslims and Christians have struggled with issues of Renaissance and Enlightenment; both have sought reform and counterreform, and sought to critique the critique of reason. Both know the challenge of pursuing intellectual integrity within the context of belief in a revealed truth. Finally, a set of issues on which Muslims and Christians have more to say to each other than either might suspect, has to do with the relationships between religion and the visual arts. Here Renaissance and Enlightenment questions converge; here the classic characterizations of Christianity as iconic and Islam as aniconic come into question and force us to rethink our understandings of how the two traditions are similar and how different with respect to the realities to which their modes of visual expression have sought to orient believers.

54. I'm surprised that you mention visual arts that way, because I've always heard that Islam is an "iconoclastic" tradition.

Islam shares the deep-seated Jewish concern over "graven images" and has never developed a tradition of religious sculpture. Even so, Muslim artists have refined a number of spectacular two-dimensional expressions of religious themes and images. Calligraphy, illumination, and illustration are the three most important.

Since there was no extensive tradition of written Arabic literature, and the Qur'an itself was all originally delivered orally, calligraphers devised a system of writing Arabic designed to insure maximum accuracy in reading and handing on the sacred text. But it was not long before talented calligraphers moved beyond the more immediately utilitarian concerns and began to create ways of beautifying manuscripts of the Qur'an. As they invented new and more attractive calligraphic styles, they started experimenting with decorative panels of floral and geometric patterns, both as frontispieces and as visual interludes between chapters of the Qur'an. To those designs they soon added text, integrating calligraphy into the geometric and vegetal creations. Panels between chapters came to include the name of the sura, the number of verses contained, and the sacred text's place of origin (either Mecca or Medina). These forms of illumination offer excellent examples of "arabesque," an infinitely repeatable pattern.

Illustration of manuscripts goes a major step beyond illumination and does not occur in manuscripts of the Qur'an. Many important religious and historical texts in a dozen major languages have appeared in lavishly executed manuscripts over the centuries. Persia, Turkey, and India have produced the best and the most numerous of these, with relatively few coming from the Arab world. Perhaps the single most important genre of illustrated manuscript from the perspective of religious studies have been that of mystical poetry created between the twelfth and sixteenth centuries. Second in importance are illustrated versions of hagiographical texts, stories of the prophets and Friends of God.

Finally, the widely held conception that Muslims don't use figural art of any kind, or that at the very least, Muslim artists never depict human beings, is not quite accurate. It is more accurate to say that Muslims never attempt to depict God visually, do not use representational art in cultic settings at all (i.e., in a mosque), rarely depict Muhammad (there are many historical examples, however), and sometimes look askance at the depiction of other religiously significant figures. A cursory glance at software for children's religious education and at books available in many mosque bookstores should be enough to dispel the general misconception about a total ban on images—they're full of illustrative drawings. And in many parts of the Islamic world, one can easily find comic and coloring books featuring famous figures from Islamic history and religious lore. The critical issue is that one not use figural imagery in an attempt either to "play God" by attempting to imitate what only God can do, or to give visual expression to what is by definition inexpressible, namely God's unity and transcendence.

55. Are there developments in religious architecture in Islamic history comparable to Romanesque, Gothic, and Renaissance architecture in Christendom?

Although the Arabic word for mosque, *masjid,* means simply "place of prostration" and denotes no particular structure, Muslims have devoted enormous attention to creating architectural contexts in which to pray. The first mosque structure of any significance was Muhammad's house in Medina, equipped with a large open-air courtyard. Within a few generations, Arab and Persian architects had begun to devise distinctive combinations of covered and uncovered space suited to Muslim ritual needs. The space generally included a covered prayer hall, an open courtyard surrounded by a covered arcade one or two aisles wide, and a minaret from which to make the call to prayer at the five specified daily times. Early mosques were relatively simple, with little exterior ornamentation. Designers gradually added small domes to accentuate the roofline of the prayer hall, and as the mosque assumed a higher profile within the cityscape, monumental decorative facades and portals displayed a beautiful face to the public. A number of the early mosques, such as those in Cordoba and Damascus, arose on the sites of earlier Christian churches, which in turn rested on the ruins of still earlier Roman temples.

As Islam became the dominant tradition in regions beyond the central Middle East and North Africa, architects began to design new forms incorporating indigenous building styles. At the center of the former Byzantine Empire, Turkish architects experimented with the hemispheric dome and half-dome as basic elements of design. With Hagia Sophia as their model, they achieved extraordinary expanses of space in their prayer halls. To accentuate both the prayer hall and the courtyard, which is typically about equal in area with the covered space, they experimented with the placement of two or more thin, graceful minarets. In Persia, the courtyard became the central unit of composition, with as many as four inward-facing facades covered in multicolored ceramic tile mosaic emphasizing the interiority favored in Persian architecture. Large, slightly bulbous tiled domes crown the prayer hall entered through one of the four inward-facing facades. Tile facing was the preferred method of enhancing the baked brick that supplied the only readily available building stock. Further east, monumental architecture developed still greater material and stylistic refinement. Architects "on loan" from Persian courts integrated the best elements of Iranian design with the finer construction materials that India had to offer—red sandstone and white marble. The results were the great mosques of the capital cities of Lahore and Delhi, and perhaps the most famous funerary monument of all time, the Taj Mahal in Agra.

From Cordoba to Kuala Lumpur and beyond, the legacy of Islamic religious architecture embraces scores of masterworks in a half dozen major styles that communicate so much about the tradition that words cannot express.

56. What are some ways of understanding how Islam has interacted with the cultures in which it has taken root?

Social scientists and theologians have recently been using the term "inculturation" to describe how religious traditions interact with their various cultural contexts. First of all, it is important to understand the circumstances under which a religious community has begun to grow in a new cultural setting. The relationship of the tradition to political and military power, and of majority to minority status, are primary variables. Second, I find it helpful to talk in terms of the complementary dynamics of Islamization and indigenization. Let me explain those terms and then I will offer some concrete examples.

By the term *Islamization* I mean the process by which the religious tradition called Islam becomes a decisive factor within a culture or ethnic group or region. By the term *indigenization* I mean the process by which a culture, ethnic group, or region confers its distinctive colors and textures on Islam. The shape of Islamdom as both unified and diverse is a function of these two processes operating at different rates in different settings.

For example, when early Muslims brought Islam into Iraq and Persia, they were in political control; but they initially made a deliberate decision to disrupt the life of the subject peoples as little as possible. As Muslims gradually became the majority, Islam became the dominant religious culture of the Middle East. Even those minority Christian communities that struggled to maintain their uniqueness came increasingly to take on cultural features originally imported by the immigrating Muslims: they learned to speak Arabic and translated their own religious concepts into Arabic, and they gradually adapted to their minority status. In other words, even non-Muslim communities in the Middle East have been Islamized to some degree.

At the same time, the way Muslims have expressed Islam in different settings has invariably been modified at least slightly by local tradition.

Even within the Middle East one finds subtle and interesting variations from one region to another—not in the basic Muslim beliefs, but in the pattern of activities readily identified as "Islamic." In Egypt, for example, intense devotion to the "Friends of God," including visitation at their tombs and exuberant celebrations of their feasts, is central to the piety of millions. A few hundred miles to the east, in Saudi Arabia, the dominant view is that such practices are entirely un-Islamic and perhaps even heretical. In other words, it is clear that Islam adapts to cultures in which it takes root.

But what about circumstances in which Muslims find themselves socially and religiously in the minority? In America, for example, the growing Muslim community faces critical and complex questions about how and to what degree they should adapt to American culture. Since the American Muslim community is made up of people from a dozen or more national and racial backgrounds, they already face the challenge of internal cultural accommodation if they are to be unified among themselves. In some areas this has led to distinct ethnic enclaves: in St. Louis, for example, there are now some five thousand Bosnian Muslim refugees, and the Detroit area is home to a very sizable Arab population. But in addition, one finds a broad range of views about, for example, how "American" Islam ought to develop. Meanwhile, slowly and almost imperceptibly, the presence of Muslims and their religious needs and values have begun to change the ways many non-Muslim Americans think and act.

57. Do Muslims sing hymns or have music when they worship?

Muslim worship is uniquely centered on the Word of God to such an extent that the spoken or "recited" word is the only sound associated with ritual prayer. In the earliest days, the call to prayer distinguished Muslim congregational practice from that of the Christian use of church bells. The call to prayer is recited in a form of chanting whose canons have become virtually universal. That is true equally for recitation of the text of the Qur'an. The word *Qur'an* means "recitation," and Muslims believe the "real" Qur'an is the one that comes to life in Arabic recitation. Two styles of recitation have become the standards. A simpler form, called *tartil* ("measured"), is used for everyday recitation of lengthier texts and moves fairly rapidly along cadences of four or five tones. A more elaborate style known as *tajwid* ("embellished") is much more majestic in pace with intervals of striking silence, is tonally more intricate, and produces a remarkably intense sound. A Qur'an reciter *(qari)* will use the latter for special occasions and situations in which only a short text is to be recited. Strictly speaking, of course, this is a type of music, but to Muslim ears it is something else altogether, the very sound of God's heavenly word.

Earthier music is an integral part of all cultures as well, and those in which Islam has played a dominant role are no exception. There is definitely such a thing as religious music, sometimes used for devotional purposes and sometimes as a more broadly entertaining medium. Devotional music is often, but not solely, associated with the paraliturgical rituals of popular religious confraternities often associated with mystical devotion. The so-called Whirling Dervishes, members of the Mevlevi order named after Mevlana ("our master") Jalal ad-Din Rumi, are perhaps the best known of such groups. Their communal prayer rituals involve a symbolic dance in which the members spin or "whirl" not only around their own axes but around the shaykh who stands in the middle. The imagery is that of the planets revolving around the sun, eternally seeking their source. Accompanying Mevlevi ritual dancing is an ensemble made up of reed flutes called neys, backed up by various kinds of plucked and bowed strings and percussions.

Virtually all of the Sufi orders have their distinctive musical ritual sessions called *sama* ("audition" or "listening"), in spite of the fact that theologians and jurists have often condemned the practice as unduly distracting and sensual. That is a testimony to music's acknowledged power over human emotions, which in turn is the principal reason why Muslims the world over continue to be enthralled by well-performed songs that develop popular religious themes, such as the wonders and virtues of the Prophet Muhammad.

58. Muslims consider the Qur'an both the epitome of Arabic literature and a work that transcends the ordinary canons of literary excellence. What role does literature play in Islamic tradition?

It is helpful first to draw a general distinction among several different kinds of Islamic religious literature. Works of a more technical type include a wide range of materials from exegetical and legal texts to theological tracts. These are typically of rather limited interest among the general public and of greater concern to specialists. Instructional and inspirational types of literature run the gamut from hagiography that enshrines the life stories of countless prophets and Friends of God, to more specialized instruction in negotiating the upward path of the spiritual quest. Each of these literary types with its various genres developed its own canons of excellence over the centuries, but in general none of them cross over into the realm of literature as a "fine art," or *belles lettres.*

Within the broad category of devotional literature we find a different situation. A great deal of the literature of piety is made up of collections of prayers and accounts of spiritual experiences, such as diaries and dream journals. But it is especially in the various genres of religious poetry that Islamic literature becomes a highly refined art form. Building on a rich tradition of Arabic lyric poetry, early Arab Muslim poets translated favored pre-Islamic metaphors of the quest for a lost love into expressions of the believer's thirst for God. The great lyricists wrote mainly in Persian and Turkish, but eventually in a host of other regional languages as well. In time there developed a breathtaking array of evocative imagery with which to allude to the ineffable relationship between seeker and Sought, lover and Beloved.

As with so many facets of the cultural expression of religious values, the relationship between literary inspiration and divine revelation has never been easy for Muslims to define precisely. Muhammad's detractors accused him of being a "mere poet," and yet subsequent tradition has pointed to the scripture's unmatched eloquence as one sign of its divine origin, developing the notion of the "inimitability of the Qur'an" as a theological principle. Scripture is therefore in a sense God's literary creation, infinitely above any product of the human imagination. But there remains an undeniable if problematic link between divine articulateness in a human tongue and the human need to express divinely inspired longings in the same language.

Classic works of religious lyric poetry remain popular among Muslims everywhere. In many parts of the world devotional poems supply both the text and inspiration for musical entertainment. Moviegoers who saw *Dead Man Walking* experienced something of the cross-cultural power of an Urdu form called *qawwali* by the intensely engaging Nusrat Fateh Ali Khan, one of Pakistan's most popular singers. Didactic religious poetry, too, retains its popularity for countless Muslims. Every Wednesday evening Muslim friends of mine welcome a small group into their home to read in Persian the *Spiritual Couplets* by the great thirteenth-century mystic Jalal ad-Din Rumi. Islamic religious poetry is alive and well and continues to play an important role in the lives of Muslims everywhere.

59. Does Islam have theologians like Augustine and Thomas Aquinas and the other great Christian thinkers?

Interest in theological questions developed very early in Islamic history. Though it is true that the interest arose out of concerns more practical than theoretical, the questions early Muslim theologians addressed nevertheless have genuinely theological implications. The oft repeated criticism that classical and medieval Muslim religious writers were limited to a defensive rehashing of the same old questions, unable to break free of the trammels of traditionalism, is on the whole no more true of the great Muslim thinkers than of their Christian counterparts. One needs always to consider the tenor of the age in question. As Christian tradition owes a great deal to its great teachers, such as Augustine and Aquinas, Islamic tradition also rests on the massive achievements of its outstanding intellectual figures. A closer look at figures like al-Ghazali, Ibn Arabi, and Ibn Taymiyya, for example, three figures every bit as important for Muslim thought as Augustine, Aquinas, and Luther for Christian, reveals a great deal of creating thinking.

Without suggesting that one can see explicit parallels between any of these Muslim and Christian figures, let me all too briefly describe why these three Muslims are important. Abu Hamid al-Ghazali (d. 1111) was born in northeastern Iran, and, showing early signs of intellectual ability, he received the best education available. His reputation for learning spread quickly and the prime minister of the Saljuqid Sultan in Baghdad invited Ghazali to head his new college *(madrasa)*. After some years of considerable success teaching religious studies, Ghazali had a sort of midlife crisis that left him experiencing considerable doubt and confusion. In a short autobiography, often compared with Augustine's *Confessions,* he describes how he embarked on a spiritual journey that led him to refocus his life. One important result was his manual of pastoral theology called the *Revitalization of the Sciences of Religion,* an itinerary of spiritual wisdom in forty sections that stretch from repentance to intimate knowledge of God.

Ibn Arabi (d. 1240) was born in the southern Iberian city of Murcia and was educated in Seville. In his twenties and thirties he traveled in North Africa to study with spiritual teachers, and at thirty-five headed for Mecca. There he began his *Meccan Revelations,* an encyclopedic and original systematic treatise of spiritual theology. Virtually every serious religious author since his time has either embraced or condemned Ibn Arabi, but almost no one has been able to ignore him.

Finally Taqi ad-Din Ibn Taymiyya (d. 1328) was a noted jurist and theologian and a reformer of sorts. Like Ibn Arabi, he generated his share of controversy, but for very different reasons; he was among those who condemned Ibn Arabi. During a career spent largely in Damascus and Cairo he sought to integrate tradition, reason, and free will in a theological synthesis, much of which he composed while in prison for views political authorities found unacceptable. Because of his posthumous association with the Wahhabi movement that supplied modern Saudi Arabia with its very strict religious ideology, Ibn Taymiyya has been unfairly written off as reactionary. He was in fact a gifted man who took his theology seriously enough to suffer for it, and whose influence and originality have yet to be fully appreciated.

60. I remember taking a college philosophy course in which there was passing reference to "the Arabian philosophers." Our textbook pretty much dismissed them as Aristotle's free ride to Europe via North Africa. Was that an accurate picture?

Your philosophy course was pretty typical in passing over a philosophical tradition that is not only deep and broad in its own right, but practically essential for a serious understanding of medieval Christian thinking. First of all, only a couple of the many significant philosophers and philosophical theologians who have called themselves Muslims were Arabs, and none actually hailed from Arabia itself. Most were of Persian or Turkic or other ethnic background. Medieval Islamic philosophers did indeed play a major role in communicating some of Aristotle's insights to European Christendom, but that is not their sole claim to our attention. More importantly, Muslim intellectuals have produced a vast body of philosophical literature that deserves to be taken seriously.

Muslim philosophical thinking began in the ninth century and continued to develop themes with important religious implications well into the seventeenth. One such theme was the relationship of revelation to reason. Theorizing about such a theologically sensitive subject naturally put some philosophers squarely in the crosshairs of religious officialdom's big guns. The most famous of these bold individuals were Ibn Sina (a.k.a. Avicenna, d. 1037), from what is now the former Soviet Central Asian republic of Uzbekistan; Ibn Rushd (a.k.a. Averroes, d. 1198), from Cordoba, a contemporary and fellow townsman of the great Jewish thinker Maimonides (d. 1204); and the Persian founder of the "Illuminationist" school, Shihab ad-Din Suhrawardi, who was executed in 1191 for thinking too boldly.

What is truly astounding about the greatest of these thinkers is that they were such multidimensional personalities and talents. Astonishingly learned, they often combined expertise in math, various physical sciences, and medicine, as well as in law—Ibn Rushd, for example, was chief judge in Cordoba. Their reputations are richly deserved and the best of them will no doubt come to be appreciated for their creativity far more than while they were alive.

61. I once heard a lecturer on the history of education claim that the first university appeared in Cairo long before the rise of the great European universities. Almost in the same breath the speaker suggested that Islam tends to be "anti-intellectual." How could those two assertions go together?

Neither statement reflects the historical realities very accurately. First of all, Muslim educational institutions do have a long and distinguished history, and in some cases they bear some similarity to those that developed in Europe during the High Middle Ages. Early Islamic religious education was relatively informal. "Circles" gathered on the floor around teaching shaykhs who sat on "chairs" in mosques, but curriculum remained largely unstructured and limited to Qur'an and Hadith, until the late tenth century. The first major institutional development occurred with the founding in 970 of the mosque called al-Azhar ("The Resplendent One"), in Cairo. At the heart of their new capital, the Fatimid dynasty began organized teaching at that mosque about 978. Since the Fatimids were an Isma'ili dynasty, the "curriculum" focused on religious issues from a Shi'i perspective.

Meanwhile further east, the Saljuqid Turks took Baghdad in 1055 and developed a type of educational institution that revolutionized higher learning in the religious sciences, the *madrasa*. Originally designed for instruction in religious law *(fiqh)*, the madrasa spread as an instrument for promulgating Sunni teaching in areas where Shi'i thought was strong. In time the *madrasa* developed broad-based religious studies curricula. Usually supported entirely by extensive charitable endowments (called *waqfs*), the great madrasas grew to encompass not only instructional facilities but residential quarters for faculty and students, libraries, liturgical space, and even social service wings housing hospitals and hostels.

In 1171 Salah ad-Din (Saladin) brought down the Fatimids and established his Ayyubid dynasty in Cairo. He and his successors transformed al-Azhar into a Sunni institution, and it became but one of many important madrasas in Cairo and across the Middle East and North Africa. Some claim al-Azhar as the "first university" in the Mediterranean world, but it developed in ways sufficiently different from the European university that one cannot trace the analogy much beyond superficial similarities.

Muslim institutions share another important feature with those of Euro-American origin: they are slow to change. But inherent conservatism is not the same as anti-intellectualism. Al-Azhar has gradually become a modern university with a broad curriculum in the arts and sciences, but its image is still largely that of a guardian of Islamic tradition against the onslaught of secularism. Though it has never had anything like the magisterial authority that the Vatican has exercised among Catholics, al-Azhar has played a similar symbolic role among Muslims. Meanwhile, in the U.S.A., a desire to preserve and hand on Islamic religious tradition has led to the growth of Muslim private education that offers interesting parallels with traditional Catholic parochial schooling.

62. I recently heard someone suggest that distorted media images of Muslims and people of Middle Eastern origin are one of the last "acceptable" public stereotypes in our society. Why don't people just lighten up with this concern for "political correctness"?

Executives and creative directors in our entertainment (and news) industry bear an enormous responsibility. So much of what people believe about others has to do with the images of those "others" that they see from day to day. Producers of mass entertainment in whatever medium face a considerable challenge in their choices as to what is appropriate in their portrayals of persons as well as in their development of story lines. Mass media play an important educational role in our society, and therefore cannot be allowed to equate profits with propriety. But how does one decide what is "proper" in entertainment imagery?

Unfortunately a simple "golden rule"—portray others only as you would like to see yourself portrayed—is not adequate here, because producers of mass media entertainment also have some responsibility to seek accuracy. But there is a fine line between the legitimate desire for historical accuracy and the unfair characterization of groups of human beings. Proportion, frequency, and intensity in the use of certain images are critical here. Survey the array of villains and plots of the top-grossing "action-adventure" films of the past ten or twenty years or so and you will come away with the powerful impression that Muslims or Arabs are ignorant, violent, and untrustworthy.

Second, propriety has a great deal to do with cultural context. Arabs, Persians, Turks, Pakistanis, to name only a few of the major ethnic groups whose members are mostly Muslim, are as richly endowed with a sense of humor as anyone. They laugh at themselves as readily as any American Christians or Jews might laugh at Steve Martin or Woody Allen. Popular soap-opera-like movies in Cairo, for example, caricature Arab bad guys mercilessly. They might even have the villains use sarcastic distortions of religious expressions such as "I seek refuge in God from the wrath of God!" And people howl at the barbs without a second thought. Transplant such caricatures into another cultural context, however, and the effect is very different.

Movie images are particularly influential in shaping our children's views of Muslims and people of Middle Eastern and Asian ancestry. That includes movies like Disney's *Aladdin* and the more recent *Kazaam.* In both cases the villains are unmistakably identified, sometimes rather subtly, with trappings most viewers would associate at least vaguely with Islam. But aren't the heroes and heroines similarly identified? In some cases, yes; but in these instances that positive identification is far outweighed by the reinforcement of negative connotations of "Muslim" and "Arab" already prevalent in our society.

SEVEN:

RELATIONSHIPS TO CHRISTIANITY AND JUDAISM

63. You mentioned earlier that Jews and Christians lived in Arabia in Muhammad's time. How did the early Muslims get along with them?

Christians lived in various parts of the Arabian peninsula and its environs during Muhammad's time. To the northwest the Arab tribe called the Ghassanids, the Byzantine buffer state against the Sasanian dynasty of Persia during Muhammad's earliest years, was Christian. To the southwest, in the Yemen, also were small Christian kingdoms. And just to the west of the Yemen, across the Red Sea, was the Abyssinian Christian kingdom of the Negus, which gave asylum to a small group of Muhammad's community in the year 615. In the city of Medina there was a significant Jewish presence as well, in three influential Jewish tribes. Muhammad's clashes with them as he shaped the new Muslim polity were, to say the least, a very grim chapter in the story of Islam's beginnings. In short, religious diversity was part of the scene in which Islam arose, and Muslim relations with the Christians were in general much less problematic than with the Jews.

The Qur'an addresses the issue of pluralism directly. Several Qur'anic texts speak of God's plan in creating the world in all its human diversity. "O humankind! We created you male and female, and we made you into peoples and tribes that you might learn to know one another. Indeed God considers the noblest among you those of most reverent awe (of God)" (Qur'an 49:13; see also 30:22, 14:4). More specifically, several texts speak of diversity in the context of plural communities of faith. God could have made humankind all of one group, but instead, left the human race composed of many segments in order to test and challenge us to work things out with each other. Frequent references to "vying with one another in good deeds" set the tone of all human, and especially religious, relationships. "We have made for each among you a revealed road [*shir'a*, related to the term *shari'a*] and a way to travel. Had God wished, he would have made you a single community, but [God wished] to test you according to what he has given each of you. Therefore vie with one another in good deeds, for God is the final goal for all of you, and it is he who will clarify for you those things about which you now argue" (Qur'an 5:48; see also 2:148 and 23:61).

Beginning with the Qur'an, Islamic tradition possesses a well-articulated attitude toward other faith communities. No other world religious scripture of the Qur'an's antiquity contains such a clearly articulated approach to this matter. It employs three terms to denote the several dimensions of human religious life. First, *din* refers to religiousness in the most general form. As a fundamental impulse that God infuses into every person, *din* has always been one and the same. It implies the basic attitude of grateful surrender in a generic sense. That original unity of human religious response ramified into different groups for a variety of reasons (see, e.g., Qur'an 2:213, 23:51–54). Even though God sent new messengers to correct the deviations that occurred through history, many people chose not to accept the corrective and kept to the old ways.

Second, the Qur'an uses the term *milla* to refer to specific religious communities that arose as a result of those deviations. Abraham, for example, was the leader of a *milla.* At various times in Islamic history, most notably during the Ottoman dynasty, the so-called millet system granted internal autonomy to individual religious groups. Finally, the overall religious entity was the Muslim *umma,* the community of believers under the tutelage of Islamic religious officialdom. While the laws of the *umma* pertained generally to the whole population, specific rules pertaining to the religious practice of the various non-Muslim communities were allowed to take precedence. For example, the central Muslim authorities respected the dietary and ritual needs of each *milla.* The overriding principle in this model is that God has allowed humankind to become religiously diverse precisely as a test, to see how well we can work out our differences, and as an impetus to a beneficial moral competition.

64. Who are the "Peoples of the Book" and how does this concept affect Islamic interreligious relations?

Judaism, Christianity and Islam come together in Islamic thought under the metaphor of "Peoples of the Book." The idea is that God has given revelations through prophets, in the form of scriptures, to more than one community of believers over the millennia. According to the Qur'an, Muslims have a special relationship to these religious communities. Especially in post-Hijra texts, the Qur'an speaks of Muslims as having much in common with the "Peoples of the Book." The term originally referred to Jews and Christians, and eventually expanded to include other communities as well, such as Zoroastrians (now commonly called Parsees). These groups were known as *dhimmis* or protected communities. And the notion that "there is no compulsion in religious matters" (*din,* Qur'an 2:256) is a central concept in Islamic views of relations with other traditions. But there is no doubt that the ultimate goal is a return to the pristine unity in which all creation worships God together. There is also no doubt that non-Muslims living in largely Muslim nations have sometimes confronted restrictions in their religious practices. The realities of interreligious relations have not always been cordial, and much difficult work needs to be done on this matter all over the world. When it comes to acceptance of diversity, all human beings have a hard time moving from theory to practice.

A charming story illustrates the ideal of interreligious openness that the Islamic traditions holds up to its members. Abraham, the paragon of hospitality, was in the habit of postponing his breakfast each day until some hungry wayfarer should happen by his house. He would then invite the stranger in to share his table. One day an old man came along. As the two were about to refresh themselves, Abraham began to pronounce a blessing. When he noted that the old man's lips formed the words of another prayer, that of a Zoroastrian, Abraham became incensed and drove the stranger away. God was displeased, and reprimanded Abraham, saying, "I have given this man life and food for a hundred years. Could you not give him hospitality for one day, even if he does homage to fire?" Abraham immediately went after the old man and brought him back home. Thus Abraham also becomes the model of openness to religious diversity. Even to the "Friend of the Merciful" *(Khalil ar-Rahman),* an honorific title of Abraham, that virtue apparently did not come naturally.

65. What did the Crusades have to do with Islam? Older books often describe the Crusades as a justifiable, even heroic, quest to liberate the Holy Land from the infidels. More recent accounts are less than flattering to the Crusaders. What do you think?

Recent research has begun to challenge older views of the Crusades by shedding new light on Islamic sources and by revealing more about Christian motives and methods. As is so often the case with military campaigns, the call to liberate the Holy Land served as a major distraction from problems at home. Crusade preaching developed into a major medieval theme to which the most persuasive of ecclesiastical orators bent their talents, promising indulgences and forgiveness of sin as well as the blessings of setting foot on sacred soil. Hope of adventure and material as well as spiritual reward were sufficient motives for thousands of warriors. From the Christian side, therefore, the Crusades were both pilgrimage and an honorable way for a young man to spend the foreseeable future.

From the Muslim side, the Crusades represented an unjustifiable declaration of all-out war on a part of the world they had ruled, even-handedly they believed, for over four hundred years. When the Muslims took Jerusalem from the weakened Byzantines in 638, they soon began to beautify the holy city. In view of the connection they saw in Muhammad's Night Journey and Ascension, they considered Jerusalem as much their Holy City as anyone else's; and they had welcomed Jewish and Christian pilgrims. Viewed from the great Muslim capitals of Cairo and Baghdad, the Crusades were not an overwhelming threat, with the exception of the initial success of the Latin Kingdom of Jerusalem (1099–1189), which resulted from the first Crusade.

But it was the countless Orthodox and other Middle Eastern Christians for whom the Crusades were perhaps most disastrous. Latin troops began the fourth Crusade by inflicting apocalyptic horrors on the Christians of Constantinople when they sacked the city during Easter of 1204. For the various smaller ancient Christian communities of the Levant, the Crusades disrupted what had for the most part settled into a reasonably peaceful status quo under Muslim rule, causing massive reprisals. That culminated in the fall of Acre to Muslim forces in 1291, an event that was a serious blow to Christian presence in, and hopes for control of, the Middle East.

66. Could you draw any parallels between developments in Islamic religious history and Christianity's ramification into Catholic and Protestant branches?

There are at least two ways to compare developments, so long as one keeps in mind that the analogies are very rough and that beneath the surface are major differences. The first method involves looking at how structures of authority developed. From the standpoint of hierarchical structure, one can loosely compare Roman Catholicism with Twelver Shi'i Islam. Both developed various ranks representing different functions and levels of authority. Early Christianity soon assigned distinctive functions to deacons, presbyters, and bishops, for example. Eventually the bishop of Rome rose to preeminence. The rank of cardinal developed, and with it the concept of the college of cardinals as the body that would elect a pope; the ranks of monsignor and archbishop, along with the various "orders" of the presbyterate (such as subdeacon and the so-called minor orders) completed the structure.

In Medieval times, Shi'i Islam also began to develop a hierarchical structure among its religious elite, singling out certain scholars as speaking with greater authority. Eventually the structure was articulated into a full-scale pyramid: God speaks through the Prophet, whose son-in-law Ali begins a line of twelve Imams. For a while in the ninth and tenth centuries, the last Imam communicated through a series of representatives; since then the chief among the upper ranks of legal scholars have assumed the authority to interpret the Word of God. And in more recent times, Shi'i legal scholars have come to be ranked according to experience, sanctity, and learning from the most highly acclaimed Ayatollahs down to the newest graduate of the theological colleges of Iran and Iraq.

Using a similar basis for comparison, Protestantism and Sunni Islam exhibit some broad similarities, as well as some important differences. In both cases the emphasis on the direct relationship of the believer to God obviated the need for intervening external structures of authority (though one could argue that functionally all ecclesiastical bodies are inherently structured to some degree). Sunni Islam has nothing like a central teaching body, although certain centers of learning, such as al-Azhar in Cairo, are regarded more highly than others.

Using another method of comparison, that of apparent historical causes, results in a very different picture. In his classic three-volume study, *The Venture of Islam: Conscience and History in a World Civilization,* the late Marshall Hodgson proposed a fascinating analogy between early sixteenth-century Protestantism in Europe and Shi'i Islam under the Safavid regime of sixteenth- and seventeenth-century Persia. To suggest but a few of many possible parallels, both developed out of sometimes chiliastic protests that had originated in the previous two centuries; both involved a strengthening of royal government; both were imposed on whole populations from above; both were at first antiaristocratic and later became associated with upper classes. In both cases, the religion of protest eventually took the form of the status quo, though the timing of the parallels is purely coincidental.

67. The Qur'an contains stories about many figures who also appear in the Bible. How are the sources similar and how do they differ?

A number of texts in the Qur'an talk about the relationships among the scriptures in general terms: "It is He [God] who sent down [revealed] to you the Book, confirming in truth all that preceded it; and before that He had sent down the Torah and the Gospel as guidance to humankind…" (Qur'an 3:3). But there are numerous other more specific connections as well. First-time readers with some knowledge of biblical narratives are invariably struck by the frequent allusions to familiar tales of Adam and Eve, Abraham, Moses, David and Solomon, Jesus and Mary.

More careful examination of the scriptures, such as a comparison of the story of Joseph in Sura 12 with the account in Genesis 37 through 50, inevitably raises numerous questions for Muslims and non-Muslims alike. When Christians and Jews discover a Qur'anic Moses or Joseph, or Jesus or Mary, who do and say things differently than in Biblical narratives, they often conclude that the Qur'an must be a corrupted "borrowing." Muslims, on the other hand, explain these discrepancies as evidence that Jews and Christians have obviously tampered with the original revelation to make it more palatable and less demanding. In fact, some argue, had the earlier "Peoples of the Book" not altered the record, God would not have needed to restore the revelation by sending Muhammad with a corrective message. Besides, Muslim tradition adds,

Muhammad was illiterate and therefore could not have plagiarized Biblical material.

Neither point of view is very helpful, for both conclusions arise rather out of a spirit of partisan competition than out of a desire to deal openly with the data of history. The arguments seek only to defend the integrity of one scripture at the expense of the other. True, a great deal is at stake here, but only to the degree that we are unable to take the larger view of God's communication with humankind.

One possibility that Christians and Jews might profitably explore is this. Just as stories of the great religious figures do not belong exclusively to any people or culture, so their capacity to reveal divine truth belongs to all whom God wishes to have access to them. Stories are a free-floating possession of humanity. If variations on narratives that some associate with the Bible occur in the Qur'an, they are there for an important purpose that transcends the rights of Christians and Jews to claim exclusive ownership of "their" stories and truths.

Muslims, for their part, might well understand the Qur'an as bringing a new perspective, reinforcing the ancient message, and enhancing and multiplying the opportunities for human beings to respond in faith. More than one Muslim author has suggested that Muhammad's "illiteracy" functions in Islamic theology much the way Mary's virginity functions in Christianity. In neither case does the human being strive to initiate. In both instances, it is God who effects the wonder of sending his word into the world. For Christians, Mary is the medium for the Word made Flesh; for Muslims, Muhammad serves as the instrument by which the Word is made Book. The "Inlibration" thus parallels the "Incarnation."

The Qur'an itself suggests an explanation for the very controversy at hand: "Humankind were once a single community. God sent prophets with news and warnings, and through them revealed the Book in truth that He might judge between people when they disagreed with one another. But, after the clear indicators had come to them, it was only out of self-centered stubbornness that they differed among themselves. God guided those who believed to the truth over which they argued, for God guides to the Straight Path whom He will" (Qur'an 2:213).

68. I know Muslims think Jesus is an important person; could you explain why? Is there an Islamic Christology?

Referred to in Arabic as Isa, Jesus appears often in the Qur'an, in a total of ninety-three verses scattered among fifteen suras. The Muslim scripture recounts several events in the life of Jesus that appear in the New Testament, but with significant differences. In addition, one finds in the Qur'an echoes of stories that appear in what Christians call apocryphal literature. A number of "signs" attest to his prophetic mission: as a youth he fashions a bird of clay and breathes life into it; he later cures a leper and a man born blind; he raises the dead by God's leave; and causes a table spread with a feast to descend from heaven for his Apostles.

Several of Jesus' Qur'anic titles are important in this context. Strictly speaking, there is and can be no Islamic "Christology," since Jesus is not the "Christ" in Muslim thought. The Qur'an refers to him eleven times as *masih,* but "messiah" here does not have the theological import that it has in Christian thought. The title "Servant of God," on the other hand, has important theological implications. It suggests that Jesus was no more than a creature, a human being, explicitly ruling out from the Muslim perspective the more expansive meanings Christians have attached to the "suffering servant" imagery of the Hebrew scriptures. The Qur'an speaks of a "Word of God" coming to Jesus, and some Muslim scholars have interpreted that to mean Jesus was the Word in that he spoke for God, or that he was "a" word because he embodied the "good news."

The Qur'an also says that God "strengthened [Jesus] with the Holy Spirit" (Qur'an 19:30–33), but the scripture argues decisively against a trinitarian concept of God. Sura 112 reads: "Proclaim: He God is One, God the eternal, He does not beget, He is not begotten, and there is none like Him." Islam also rejects the idea that Jesus died by crucifixion, arguing that a look-alike (possibly Simon of Cyrene or an apostle) was crucified in his stead. The import of the Qur'an's treatment of the final events in Jesus' life seems to be that God caused him to ascend after his apparent death. Tradition has it that Jesus will return at the end of time to vanquish the anti-Christ and usher in an age of justice. After forty years Jesus will die and be buried in Medina with Muhammad, then rise in the general resurrection along with the rest of humankind.

69. Does Mary also have a place in Islamic tradition?

Mary occupies a very important position in Muslim sacred history. She is, first of all, the mother of a prophet and thus worthy of high honor in keeping with the role God chose for her. Sura 19 of the Qur'an is named after Mary and she is mentioned more often by name in the Muslim scripture than in the Christian scripture. Sura 19 and other Qur'anic texts include a number of parallels to scenes recorded in Biblical texts, but almost always with very interesting differences. No other woman is mentioned by name in the Qur'an. Mary's own birth is miraculous and Zachary looks after her in her youth. A "spirit of God" in human form, whom later tradition identifies as Gabriel, visits Mary and "breathes" the Word into her garment and she hastens to "a remote place" for shame at her unmarried pregnancy. There she gives birth while clinging to a palm tree for support. As she shakes the tree in labor it showers her with fresh ripe dates. Invited to eat her fill, she chooses to fast and to keep silence through the day, a "fast of silence" that later Muslim mystical poets would interpret as her call to think of nothing but God. When relatives accuse her unjustly, the infant Jesus speaks up in her defense. The principal difference between Muslim and Christian views is that since Islam does not consider Jesus divine, Mary is not the mother of God.

Popular lore ranks Mary among the "four most beautiful" women God created. Also called the "best of the world's women," the four include Asiya, martyred wife of the Pharaoh of Moses' time; Muhammad's first wife, Khadija; and Fatima, the daughter of Muhammad and Khadija. There are a number of interesting parallels between Mary and the roles of other women in popular Islamic piety. Like Asiya, who "adopted" the infant Moses, Mary was the mother of a prophet. Sunni tradition accords Fatima special status partly because of her mourning for the loss of her father; in Shi'i tradition, especially, her grief at the loss of her martyred sons makes Fatima, like Mary, the "Lady of Sorrow." And on a popular level, some Shi'i Muslims consider Fatima a "perpetual" virgin in spite of being the wife of Ali and mother of Hasan and Husayn.

Tradition regards Mary and Jesus as the only two human beings born without the "touch of Satan" that makes newborn infants cry. Mainstream tradition has denied Mary and all other women the status of prophethood; but it is worth noting that at least one historically important religious scholar, Ibn Hazm of Cordoba (d. 1064), held that Mary did indeed receive the revealed message that makes one a prophet *(nabi)*, even though she did not receive the full status of "messenger" *(rasul)* accorded to a number of prophets. Mary's spouse, Joseph, does not appear in the Qur'an, but traditional lore includes him along with most of the scenes in which Joseph participates in the New Testament.

70. Do Muslims have rituals like confirmation, bar and bat mitzvah, or circumcision? Are there any other kinds of ritual whose general intent the three traditions share?

All religious traditions seek to offer their members assistance in getting through important or difficult experiences in life by means of "rites of passage." These practices vary to some degree from one culture to another, but there is generally a common core in the rituals. Confirmation and bar/bat mitzvah observances are examples of initiatory rites, celebrations of a formal religious welcoming into the community. Islam also has its initiatory rites. On the seventh day a child's hair is shaved and some parents give its weight in currency to the poor. At that time a father might whisper the *adhan* or call to prayer into the child's right ear and the *iqama* (the invitation to begin prayer that is announced once worshipers gather in the mosque) into the left ear. Formal naming occurs in this context as well, with preference given to names traditionally associated with outstanding Muslims, beginning of course with Muhammad.

Muslims also practice a rite of circumcision, but age and ritual circumstances vary regionally. In some places it is an actual puberty rite; in others infants are circumcised. Feast days of Friends of God are often favorite occasions for the circumcision of older individuals especially. Their initiation is thereby associated with the *baraka*, blessing and grace, bestowed in connection with the powerful presence of the saint.

Fasting is another important ritual link among the three traditions. Jews recognize a number of day-long fasts through the year, the most important being Yom Kippur (Day of Atonement) and the Ninth of Av (mourning the destruction of the Temple) on which participants fast from sunset to sunset. Other occasions commemorate tragic events in Jewish history or function as preparatory rites, such as the days immediately preceding festive Purim or Passover. Christians traditionally think of the forty days of Lent as a time of fasting, but the observance is generally marked by partial rather than complete fasting through the day and in recent times has become somewhat relaxed in its demands. The Muslim fast through the thirty days of Ramadan extends across a shorter period, but calls on participants to fast altogether from dawn to sunset. The three traditions recommend fasting for a variety of similar reasons, but Judaism is unique in its observance of specific occasions of historic tragedy.

71. If Judaism, Christianity, and Islam are "family" to the degree that they claim Abraham as their father in faith, why don't we understand each other better?

Even though members of the same family don't always get along, one would think that religious communities that all trace their lineage back to Abraham could find at least a little to agree on. Paradoxically, the potential of family membership for fostering a sense of unity and mutual understanding is rivaled only by its potential for divisiveness.

On the one hand, the classical Islamic understanding of the familial connection represents a highly developed position on interreligious relations. Because Islam's scripture came after those of Judaism and Christianity, the Qur'an addresses the challenges of relations with Jews and Christians directly. On the other hand, the same classical doctrine implies that Muslims know "true" Christianity or Judaism better than Christians and Jews. Islam teaches that Jews and Christians have, over the centuries, progressively lost touch with the essence of their revelations, and so suffered an alienation from their truest religious selves. This is so because "true" Christianity or Judaism in their original, uncorrupted forms, were identical with the fundamental teachings of Islam.

Two major problems in positing or presuming a familial relationship are: first, that, as in all families, the relationship is not chosen but seen as a fact of life; and second, that, as in all families, there are skeletons in the closet. One can respond to the first either by agreeing to work with the actual situation by deciding to make the best of an unpleasant situation, or by acting out one's resentment of it. All three modes of responding to the problem of an unasked-for familial relationship involve communication. Acting out or other forms of passive-aggressive behavior are notoriously difficult to combat because their inherent designs for sabotage occur together with an avowed desire to cooperate.

Another problem that plagues many families is that of "skeletons in the closet." A story told long ago by the Persian poet Nizami (d. 1209) in his splendid mystical epic, *Seven Portraits,* offers a solution.

Once upon a time, King Solomon married the queen of Sheba. Together they had a child who was ill from birth. The child's health became so worrisome to the parents that they feared for its life. They begged God to heal the languishing tot and vowed that they would do anything God asked if only their child could be healed. Came the divine message: reveal to one another your deepest secret and your child will begin to recover forthwith.

Bilqis, queen of Sheba, searched her soul and admitted to Solomon that she still harbored resentment over one thing he had done to her. Solomon had once tricked her into lifting the hem of her skirt by requiring her to walk across a floor so glossy she would think it was covered with water. The King had heard the queen walked on cloven hooves and wanted to find out discreetly if the rumor were true. Still, Bilqis confessed, she yearned to trick Solomon back for his perfidy.

Solomon for his part admitted that, wealthy and powerful as he was, and as far-reaching as was the arm of his sovereignty—now including even the lands of Sheba as well as all the animal kingdoms—he nevertheless wanted more. Yes, he was indeed greedy and not quite content with the extent of his dominion. The moment the royal couple had brought their dark secrets into the light, their child began to heal.

Which is the Christian and which the Muslim, I leave to your imagination. What is abundantly clear is that we each have tucked away some embarrassing little secrets about our feelings toward the other; but it is equally clear that we hide them far less effectively than we imagine. The destructive energies of our thinly veiled real feelings, fears, and suspicions inevitably manifest themselves, taking shape indirectly in our social and cultural institutions. As people entrusted with the care and nurturance of the human race and the planet, we can see—if we are honest—that bad communication hurts posterity and that the wounds of one generation are incarnated in the next.

72. Given all of these connections and acknowledging that we are members of the same large family, at least in a general way, what is a good first step toward better relations?

In the story of Solomon and Bilqis, healing came only after the two could admit their deepest secrets. What must Christians and Muslims admit to one another? What does one hear Muslims and Christians saying among themselves, beneath the expressed, positive and well-intentioned awareness that we must learn to live together?

A Christian Secret: I am afraid of you. So many public statements in response, for example, to Salman Rushdie make me feel like Muslims are fanatical and that they will kill anyone who happens to express an opinion that goes against the views of Muslims. Is it just a show to make non-Muslims think that Muslims have such great reverence for their Prophet? Or do even the most mild-mannered Muslims really feel such personal insult at the opinions of a novelist that they must call for his death?

A Muslim Secret: I am suspicious of you. Though I may never have lived where Christian missionaries sought, by whatever means, to convert my brothers and sisters, I cannot shake the hunch that if you approach me in a friendly way, it is because you really want me to deny my faith. I find it very difficult to believe that you want to learn about Islam without undermining and discrediting my beliefs.

A Christian secret: I don't understand why you insist that we Christians have corrupted our scripture and our tradition. On the one hand I know that Christians have often failed to live up to the demands of what we believe to be our divinely inspired scriptures, but, on the other, I resent the implication that the Christian tradition is little more than half-truths and downright lies.

A Muslim secret: I am hurt at your refusal to accept even the possibility that God sent Muhammad to restore truth to the world. I understand that for you such a claim would mean that Jesus was no longer the final and definitive messenger. And I hear you say you fear that Islam wants to swallow up or negate all other traditions. Still, this standoff bothers me because we seem to be staring each other down, each waiting for the other to blink.

In the end, what Christians and Muslims really need to say to each other is this: Please do not judge me by consigning me to the anonymity of a mass of humanity labeled "all Muslims" or "all Christians." In the American print and electronic media one all too often senses the tendency to conclude that all Muslims are potential terrorists or that Islamic fundamentalism is inherently linked to violence. When did you last hear a suspect in a criminal investigation referred to as a six-foot, two-hundred-pound, blonde-haired Christian? Although an American might cite fewer examples of parallel Muslim characterizations of Christians, I have spoken to several immigrant Muslims who have expressed a fear that there must surely be Christians other than David Koresh or members of Aryan groups who have well-stocked arsenals and are prepared for a violent end of history. Not long ago in St. Louis, the celebrated and protracted trial of members of the Moorish Science Temple caused some difficulty for local Muslims, even though the Temple's association with mainstream Islam is marginal at best. Television viewers saw the grand shaykh of the temple proclaim in no uncertain terms that his arrest and conviction resulted from no less than a global conspiracy to discredit Islam and Muslims. We face a serious challenge to improve our communications with each other.

73. Could you give an example of successful Christian-Muslim dialogue? What do people talk about in dialogue groups and what lessons have their members learned thus far?

In 1980, a successful Muslim-Christian dialogue group developed in Milwaukee. In its scores of meetings over the years, the group has included between twenty and twenty-five members, about one-third Muslim and two-thirds Christian from several denominations. Emphasizing the need to understand the other party as that party wishes to be understood, the group seeks to listen and to teach, to pass along to their coreligionists the fruits of their dialogue, to focus on human dignity, and to promote educational endeavors designed to break down stereotypes. Proselytizing has no place in the dialogue group.

Among its activities, the Milwaukee group has held a peace prayer service and took part in a study of history textbooks used in the city's elementary schools, looking for biases and stereotypes. The Milwaukee group has benefited from a stable core membership over the years. Visitors and guests often attend, but the presence of a long-term core group keeps the level of discussion advancing and avoids the need for continual backtracking and reestablishment of ground rules.

Perhaps the most fundamental lesson is an appreciation of doctrinal similarities and differences. Once participants come to know each other better, what may have begun as a kind of technical catechismlike exchange can become a more personal reflection on how each member has internalized the basic beliefs. Included here, but perhaps approachable at a more advanced stage, is that very delicate matter of acknowledging built-in theological positions that can prejudice or even sabotage dialogue: in particular, the Christian view of its revelation as final, and the classic Muslim view that the once pure message at the heart of Christianity and Judaism became corrupt and in need of definitive restatement.

A second major lesson concerns the matter of honesty about personal attitudes over the long haul in dialogue. Here one finds acknowledgment of the importance of simply meeting one another in breaking down stereotypes, of the need for patience and persistence, of letting go the desire to see the other change, of willingness to risk putting one's fears on the table, of willingness to be misunderstood and be told one does not understand. All such matters demand a considerable level of personal security, maturity, and freedom, since they touch on issues potentially very threatening.

Finally, there are a number of lessons that one could group under the heading of cultural sensitivities. Although it is probably impossible ultimately to separate religious concerns neatly from geopolitical concerns, Muslim-Christian dialogue requires some ability to distinguish truly American issues that bear directly on the interaction of the participants, from international matters. Obviously, American involvement in the Middle East and elsewhere, for example, is hardly negligible; but participants need to be aware of how such issues can drive wedges between American participants of both religions.

A related lesson concerns the need for sensitivity to various practices, including an awareness of dietary restrictions and ritual needs. Social occasions should include alternatives to pork and to alcoholic beverages. During the month of Ramadan, non-Muslims might be especially sensitive about whether they will serve refreshments during daylight hours, when fasting Muslims would not be able to share the food.

Ritual needs are a second major category. Gatherings should take into account daily Muslim times of ritual prayer, enabling Muslims who wish to pray to do so. Christian dialogue partners and planners ought to familiarize themselves with the current year's religious calendar and be aware of when the sacred observances and festivities of the Muslim lunar schedule will fall.

74. Can you suggest other models for interreligious dialogue and their various advantages and disadvantages?

Several models come to mind. First there is interaction between "official" representatives of the traditions on a local level: priest or minister, rabbi, and imam. The advantage is that participants exercise leadership roles and can bring the message home to parish church, synagogue, and mosque. There are two disadvantages. One is that levels of religious education and intellectual sophistication may vary greatly and lead to frustrated expectations concerning the quality and tone of the exchange. In addition, where a Catholic is involved, a priest may regard himself as speaking in some way for the whole church, while the imam plays no such official role in Islam. The challenge in this model is that of persuading prospective partners that the discussion is not about winning and losing, or even scoring points, but about increasing mutual understanding.

On an academic level, discussion about the interpretation of texts and about theological issues already occurs, but in a nondialogical way, at academic conferences. While this allows for a relatively free and unprejudiced exchange of ideas, it tends to be rather clinical and does not deal with beliefs at the level of experience and faith. Here the challenge is to keep in mind that the ideal of academic objectivity does not exempt participants from trying to be sensitive to the other's beliefs.

Parent-to-parent dialogue raises interesting possibilities. A more pastoral kind of conversation has already begun all over the country, wherever Muslims and Christians discover that their children attend the same schools, for instance. Common concerns over values in education can lead to further and more personal sharing of faith, of the experience of God's action in the world, and of diverse ways of celebrating religious convictions. Such conversation can occur, for example, as a result of memberships in school or neighborhood organizations. They have the advantage of bringing people together within the scope of a common project that demands cooperation and mutual respect. On the other hand, people may not have the time to allow their conversations to move beyond the more immediate issues, or may be embarrassed to ask questions about others' beliefs, or may be afraid to admit their ignorance. The challenge here is to persuade people that mutual understanding of religious values is just as important to the future of their neighborhoods and schools as getting the sidewalk fixed or making sure the cafeteria serves healthy food.

Finally, high school and college courses of various kinds can offer an excellent forum for introducing students to each other's faiths and cultural backgrounds. A major advantage is that younger students especially have a natural curiosity about their peers from other backgrounds. A disadvantage is that it may be difficult for some students to admit that they have not kept in touch with their faith communities. Sometimes poorly informed partners in conversation can actually reinforce stereotypes about their own traditions. The challenge therefore is to foster genuine openness and get around the implicit threat of differences between cultures and belief systems.

Possible themes for dialogue might include: search for common ground in matters of belief (scriptures; the role of prophets; major images of God; the place of Muhammad, Jesus, and Mary, mother of Jesus); and responses to questions of environment, family life, education, neighborhood, and works of mercy.

EIGHT:

WOMEN AND FAMILY

75. What sort of role models does Islamic tradition offer to young women?

Islamic tradition is rich with stories of exemplary individuals. As in the Christian and other traditions, the men far outnumber the women, but there are many prominent Muslim women who model faith and virtue. Foremost among them is Fatima, daughter of Muhammad and his first wife, Khadija, who died when Fatima was quite young.

Fatima is best known as the wife of Ali and mother of Husayn and Hasan, the first two Shi'i martyr-imams. Hadith accounts do not gloss over the difficult times Fatima experienced with her husband, with Muhammad himself acting as arbiter in their disputes. But she fought against Abu Bakr (the first caliph, by Sunni reckoning) for Ali's right to succeed Muhammad. More recently, several Muslim scholars, male and female, have interpreted Fatima as the paradigm of the liberated woman as exemplified by her independent thinking and courage in adversity.

In traditional and popular sources, however, Fatima appears as the utterly devoted wife. Stories about Fatima have been told in many languages and cultural settings throughout the history of Islam. As one might expect, some features of her life and experience remain fairly constant whenever and wherever Muslims have recounted her life. But Fatima also takes on the characteristics of every culture that preserves her memory. In other words, she is a model held up for the emulation of Muslim women of every age; but her image is also shaped by the values of each society in that she becomes a reflection of a society's prevalent image of the "ideal" woman. The Fatima of Swahili epic poetry is rather different from the Fatima of Persian Shi'i literature or North African popular lore. One can observe the same sort of cultural reinterpretation in stories of the Virgin Mary, for example: Christians may discern a very similar message underlying all of her claimed apparitions, but the Lady of Guadalupe is different from the Lady of Medjugorje in ways that go beyond clothing style.

121

76. Do women have a place in the Islamic view of human rights?

An area of Islamic human rights that non-Muslims have often cited in recent times as problematical is the place of women in society. Outsiders frequently fault Muslims for their failure to foster the social equality that would allow women to pursue careers outside the home. As a prime example, some critics point to the recent arrest of a number of Saudi women who violated a ban on driving automobiles. But if "Islam" is the operative value system in this instance, one must ask why in so many other predominantly Muslim countries all over the world most women do not wear veils and are free to drive cars. In nearby Jordan numbers of women now study in Shari'a schools once open only to men. Actual practices in relation to these and other similar social issues are clearly too complex and variegated to be explained by reference to Islamic religious injunctions, especially those that seem to be country or region specific.

One has to keep a number of factors in mind when presuming to judge other cultural and religious systems. First, no humanly devised social structure is perfectly just, and that includes those that claim divine sanction. Second, all cultures and societies have their unchallenged assumptions, and are subject to a certain amount of upheaval when those assumptions are challenged. Third, one cannot simply impose one's own preferences on another culture. Cultural differences come about as close to an absolute value as anything in human experience and add a richness and diversity to life on earth. One should not therefore simply transplant into other cultural settings everything that Americans think essential to a free and just society. Though there may be a fine line between certain unquestioned practices in a given society and violations of human rights, outside observers have the duty to look for that line and not simply assume those under scrutiny have crossed it. Finally, Muslim women in many nations continue to work together for the improvement of conditions for all their sisters and brothers.

77. During the Gulf War I heard that Saudi women are not allowed to drive cars, and now the Taliban in Afghanistan have forbidden women to work outside the home. Is there some official prohibition on women having a public place in society? And what about educational opportunities?

In many societies across the world Muslim women occupy a wide variety of positions in business and the professions, from banking and engineering to health care and social services. There are also areas in which those who hold political power continue to exercise rigid social control by severely limiting the options available to women, invariably claiming Qur'anic sanction for their policies. In some cases the practices that now appear to outsiders as backward and oppressive arose as a reaction to western colonialism as a way of protecting Muslim women from the countless ill effects of the unwanted intrusion, and as a way of keeping families intact. But what about the strong evidence that many Muslim women do not enjoy social equality with men? How much of that is "Islamic"? It is virtually impossible to separate religious sanction from deeply ingrained cultural values. But it is helpful to observe the wide variations in the status of women from one culture to another.

It is also important to keep in mind that even in the most "liberated" societies it is not always perfectly clear what constitutes genuine freedom. Many Muslims, men and women, sincerely believe that what passes for freedom and gender equality in some cultural settings is far more demeaning than what they perceive in their own systems as responsible and necessary protective measures. In many traditional societies, including some with predominantly Islamic populations, women have not enjoyed equal educational opportunities for the simple reason that their roles as traditionally understood neither required nor allowed time for education. This is changing, slowly in most places but rather dramatically in a few, and it will in time become clearer to Muslim and non-Muslim observers alike that a world of educated women is not only compatible with Islam but virtually demanded by its emphasis on human dignity.

78. What about female circumcision? Is it widely practiced? And does it have anything really to do with Islamic teaching?

Female circumcision, or clitoridectomy, is still practiced in some societies, and some of those are predominantly Muslim. But the practice is not originally or inherently Islamic and is best understood in cultural rather than religious terms. The Qur'an does not mention clitoridectomy at all, and the Hadith mention it rather briefly by way of ruling out any but the most minimal form of it. Islamic law sources list the practice as recommended, rather than required, but for reasons of custom rather than religion. In many societies, "custom" includes the belief that clitoridectomy is necessary to protect a young woman's virginity, virtue, fertility, and marriageability. Because the practice represents such a clear attempt at social control, a number of contemporary feminist writers, both Muslim and non-Muslim, have targeted clitoridectomy and all other forms of female genital mutilation as inhumane and both morally and religiously indefensible. Some countries with large Muslim populations have officially outlawed the practice, while in others, including the religiously conservative Saudi Arabia, custom has ruled it out more informally.

79. We hear a lot about "family values" these days. Are there distinctively Islamic family values?

Traditional Muslim views on family emphasize the understanding of clear roles for husband and father, wife and mother, and children. "Family" means different things from one society and culture to another, but it is reasonably safe to say that in most societies where Muslims constitute majorities or large minorities, people think of family as extended rather than nuclear. As Muslim populations grow in Europe and the Americas over the next several generations, it will be very interesting to see to what extent Muslim families are influenced by the dominant understanding of nuclear family.

One of the earliest Qur'anic correctives to a serious problem in pre-Islamic family custom is its condemnation of the burying of unwanted children, especially girls, alive. The scripture also accorded women a number of clear rights and responsibilities not previously acknowledged in Arabian custom. In addition to limiting the number of wives allowed to one man, the Qur'an secured many improvements in the lot of women. It stipulates that a wife is entitled to personal ownership of money and goods—the dower went directly to her rather than to her male guardian, as was previously the practice. It also provides for the termination of a marriage under certain circumstances, and for a woman's entitlement to a set portion of inheritance. Scripture does not unequivocally mandate veiling and seclusion, but does allow a woman to retain her name and guarantees her privacy. In some respects Islam as a religious and ethical code established men and women on a remarkably equal footing.

By tradition and custom, women have almost universally stood at the center of the Muslim family. In addition, Muslim law includes extensive development of family issues such as inheritance, divorce, and child custody. For example, women generally get custody of younger children, but after puberty children usually stay with the father on the assumption that he will be better able to provide for their increasing financial needs. On the whole, the husband clearly has the greater legal advantage, in spite of efforts by reformers in this century to find a balance. Opposition to change in the law of personal status has often gone hand in hand with resistance to residual colonialism and a desire not to accommodate too readily to influences perceived as "Western."

80. Can Muslims get divorced? Do they have to go through the same legal procedures as other Americans if they live here?

Islamic tradition has always recognized and allowed for divorce under certain specific circumstances, although according to tradition, God considers divorce the most hateful of all licit acts. Husband and wife can divorce by mutual consent, a relatively simple procedure. A wife can also initiate a divorce proceeding for cause, including a variety of marital "defects," among which are impotence, apostasy, and insanity. A husband can divorce his wife by means of a triple repudiation in a process that ordinarily takes several months. He must wait three menstrual periods to ascertain that his wife is not pregnant, pronouncing the repudiation each month. If she is pregnant, he must wait for a period after the child is born. The couple can reconcile if the husband does not complete the three repudiations. In some countries, authorities have sought to provide further safeguards for women by situating the practice firmly within a juridical context. Syrian law discourages easy repudiation by requiring husbands to continue support to a wife for at least a year after divorce. Muslims who live in the U.S.A. must also abide by civil law in obtaining a legal divorce.

81. Do Muslim parents choose their children's marriage partners?

Many Muslim families both here and abroad continue to pursue ancient cultural tradition when it comes to choosing spouses for their marriageable children. Some parents will even take out "classifieds" in the "matrimonials" feature of magazines like *Islamic Horizons,* published in Malaysia but distributed in a U.S.A. version. Each edition includes several dozen ads by parents seeking inquiries for both sons and daughters. Ads include much of the sort of information you might expect—age, height, references to physical attractiveness, and desired personal qualities such as intelligence and honesty—as well as the often expressed concern that the prospective partner be a devout Muslim. Not all Muslims adhere to this mode of marriage preparation, whether or not assisted by the printed page, even in predominantly Muslim countries. But many still regard it as the best way to guide their children and avoid the hit-and-miss approach that they see as typical of the nontraditional American way of courtship.

82. Do Muslims marry outside their faith? How do they deal with "mixed marriages"?

After his first wife died, Muhammad himself married Christian and Jewish women. At least one important Qur'anic text addresses the issue and allows the Prophet the liberty to do so (5:5). Some of the women became Muslims; some did not. Many historians consider Muhammad's practice the exception rather than the rule, justifiable in the interest of social reconstruction and establishing necessary "political" alliances. Later Islamic history records some significant examples of prominent Muslim rulers marrying non-Muslim women, including Hindus and others not clearly included among the "People of the Book." Majority opinion among the classic legal schools holds that, though it is a less than ideal situation, Muslim men may marry non-Muslim women, but not the reverse.

83. Do Muslims practice polygamy?

The practice of polygamy—or more precisely, polygyny, marriage to "many women"—in the Middle East predates Islam by many centuries, with several major biblical figures (Abraham, David, Solomon) among the most celebrated polygynists. With Islam came a systematic regulation of the practice in the Arabian peninsula. The Qur'an states fairly unambiguously that a man may marry up to four wives, so long as he can treat them all equally, both materially and emotionally (4:3): "Marry women of your choice, two, three, or four; but if you are concerned that you may not be able to treat them justly, then only one...." Special Qur'anic dispensation allowed Muhammad to exceed that limit by reason of his responsibilities as leader of an increasingly complex social entity. Early practice of polygyny had the social advantage of providing a place of refuge for unattached women who would find it virtually impossible to survive on their own. Times of war were especially perilous for the wives and children of men who had gone off to battle. Muhammad himself and a number of his Companions are said to have married widows under such circumstances.

In recent times, polygyny has been either outlawed or tightly controlled in many Muslim nations. One of the arguments against it has been that although in complex contemporary societies a man might manage material equality, emotional and psychological equity is no longer possible. Even in the Qur'an one finds the suggestion that beyond the material realm, such equal treatment is very difficult in practice: "You will not be able to treat the wives with equality, however much you desire that. Do not turn away entirely, leaving her in suspense" (Qur'an 4:129). For any number of reasons, the vast majority of Muslims simply assume that monogamy is the only feasible marriage practice. Polygyny is now strictly regulated in a number of Muslim countries, so that few men would actually be able to meet the legal requirements. Some modern authors, such as Muhammad Abduh (1849–1905), have argued that Muslims can no longer consider polygyny an option, interpreting the Qur'an's warning verse (4:129 cited above) as a virtual prohibition. Various surveys of Muslim women suggest that they are almost unanimous in stating a preference for monogamy.

84. It's easy to get the impression that Muslim women have a much harder time than non-Muslim American women being recognized as independent and capable. Why is that impression so prevalent?

Possibly because of reports about the fate of so many women in Afghanistan after the takeover by the Taliban revolutionaries; or media images of Middle Eastern, especially Iranian, women covered from head to toe apparently participating in anti-American or anti-Western demonstrations. Whatever the reason, I would emphasize that the oppression of women is not a distinctively Islamic issue. While it is undoubtedly true that Muslims have often used religion to control social behavior in various contexts, Muslims are not alone in acting thus. The roots of the clearly subordinate social status of women evidenced in numerous societies today—including, some would argue, our own—go much deeper and are much more ancient than Islam or any other system of religious values.

A basic problem has always been how to interpret an ancient scripture in modern times. The Qur'an's teachings about women were enormously progressive in their original historical context. Women's legal and financial rights saw dramatic advances over pre-Islamic social norms. Since Muslims generally understand the Qur'an to be eternally valid and universally applicable, the desire to implement Qur'anic teachings here and now is perfectly understandable. The hypothetical question of whether a twentieth-century revelation would be identical with a seventh-century revelation, or call for similar advances over current social values, always stirs interesting discussion.

Traditional Islamic values include a very clear picture of gender roles, especially within the family. But the predominant view is that in order to maintain family order, the husband and father has the final say in matters of dispute and has the authority to discipline when necessary.

85. I'm a little confused about the practice of wearing veils. Does Islam require it or not?

Nowhere does the Qur'an specify that women are to wear veils. It merely stipulates that women dress modestly at all times. However, in some societies female modesty has been judged to include covering the face to varying degrees, even so far as to using a semi-see-through veil that doesn't even have openings for the eyes. In very traditional areas all over the Middle East and North Africa, for example, one is still likely to see veiled women. But in places like Indonesia or Malaysia, and the United States, some Muslim women wear full-length robes and head scarves when they are in public or when any but women friends or their closest male relatives visit them in their homes.

Many non-Muslims look disapprovingly on Muslim women who choose to "cover" themselves, regarding them as reactionary or hyperconservative. Like the rest of us, most Muslims would rather be judged by their character than by external appearances. It is important to appreciate how Muslims understand the primary intent of traditional teaching about such things as modest clothing, for both men and women: respect for the human dignity of each person. Many Muslims think some contemporary societies, including our own, show little respect for women. So much advertising makes it clear that women's bodies are either the commodity for sale or the chief enticement in marketing another product. It is hardly surprising that some Muslims seek support in their religious tradition for a more humane and dignified treatment of women.

NINE:

GLOBAL AND GEOPOLITICAL ISSUES

86. Is Islam the fastest growing religion in the world? Where are the largest concentrations of Muslim populations? Are most Muslims Arabs? What other aspects of world Muslim population are helpful in understanding Islam?

Among global religious communities, Islam does seem to show the fastest rate of growth, with Christianity running a close second. In total numbers, Christians still appear to outnumber the one billion Muslims by four or five hundred million. The largest concentrations of Muslims by geographical region are in South Asia, with around a third of the world's total in Pakistan, India, and Bangladesh. Combining all of the Muslims in the Middle East and Africa adds more than another third. And the populations of Indonesia, the nation with the largest number of Muslims, combined with those of the rest of East, Central, and Southeast Asia comprise roughly the final third.

Principal nations with majority Muslim populations include virtually all of the Middle Eastern and North African countries, plus a couple of sub-Saharan African states such as Nigeria; Pakistan and Bangladesh; Malaysia and Indonesia; and the five Central Asian republics formerly belonging to the Soviet Union (Kazakhstan, Tajikistan, Kirghizia, Uzbekistan, and Turkmenia). Dozens of other nations include significant minority populations, with India's over one hundred million Muslims at the head of the list. Another important minority we rarely hear about is that of the People's Republic of China.

The total number of Arab Muslims is roughly equivalent to that of Indonesians alone, about one-sixth of the world total. Across North Africa one finds also Muslims who are ethnic Berbers. People of Indic background are by far the largest single group, if one considers a large number of ethnic subgroups together. Turkic descent accounts for the lineage of most of the citizens of Turkey as well as those of the former Soviet Central Asian republics and a region once called Eastern Turkestan that now makes up a large area of Western China. The people of Iran and Afghanistan are largely of Indo-Aryan descent and are more closely related ethnically to the people of the Indian subcontinent than they are to their Arab or Turkic neighbors.

Muslims speak and write in dozens of major language groups. Arabic remains the chief Islamic language, not because many Muslims speak it but because it is the language of the Qur'an and is thus associated with Islam's sacred origins. Multiple languages and dialects of Turkic, Indic (such as Urdu, Sindhi, and Gujerati) and Indo-European (such as Persian), Malayo-Polynesian, and African origin remain important for careful study of Islam.

87. I recently heard Islam characterized as the next major threat to "Western" civilization, the new Evil Empire that will succeed Communism. Sounds like a major oversimplification, but could you comment on it?

At the risk of oversimplification in the other direction, I would respond that, alas, every society needs its Evil Empire. When no obvious candidate fills the bill, we will conjure one up in the vain hope that somehow it will make us feel better about ourselves. During the past couple of decades there has been much talk about "resurgent Islam," fueled by such events as the Iranian Revolution, the Palestinian Intifada, and the ascendancy of the Afghan Taliban. Books with titles like *The Islamic Bomb: The Nuclear Threat to Israel and the Middle East* (1982) raise the specter of some sort of nuclear conspiracy, as though Islam represented a unitary political will intent on world domination. In fact, "Islam" is nothing quite like the various "isms" one can realistically imagine bringing political and economic resources to bear on some global or even regional objective—capitalism, communism, colonialism, imperialism, or—on a smaller scale—Zionism, for example.

On the other side of that coin, neither is "the West" anything like a unified secularist bloc of political, economic, and cultural determination, set adamantly against the real or imagined religio-moral fervor of "the East." Still, it is much easier to construe the world as neatly defined opposing forces than to come to terms with the common humanity that underlies all our differences. Muslims are on the whole just about as susceptible to these kinds of generalizations as non-Muslims, however, and are often coresponsible for perpetuating the sweeping dichotomy.

In short, Islam as a religious tradition is in no way a threat to world peace and order. On the contrary, it is as important a force for maintaining peace and order as any other tradition.

88. Many people—including Muslims—have the impression that Muslims are all alike in the way they approach their religion. Can you comment on that?

Members of the same religious tradition seem to cherish the idea of unity in their ranks for positive reasons ("We all believe the same things"), even as outsiders often use similar observations for the purpose of dismissing others ("They're all alike"). Neither side is quite correct. From the earliest days there has been a variety of ways of understanding what it is to be a Muslim, even beyond the variations in "denomination" (Sunni/Shi'i) and legal methodology (the various "schools of law"). Let me describe four "religio-cultural styles" of Islam.

If one's only acquaintance with Muslims came via the news media, one might think that all Muslims were "radical fundamentalists." Unfortunately, when non-Muslims hear the term *fundamentalist* so used, they often translate it as "lunatic fringe." Perhaps the term *revivalist* is better suited here; scholars have recently begun to use the terms *integralist* and *islamist* to describe this style. By whatever name, its general characteristics are a literalist reading of the Qur'an, whose absolute validity remains pure, universal, and unconditioned by historical circumstances. Often assumed to be rigidly traditional, this style has, ironically, often encouraged highly original and imaginative scriptural exegesis, and virtually demands the exercise of independent investigation *(ijtihad)* in the elaboration of law. Politically activist, the approach seeks to recapture the spirit of the golden age of the Prophet and adapt it to contemporary needs, thereby establishing a society purged of centuries of irrelevant medieval interpretation and of "western secularist" influences that have sidetracked Muslims from their original destiny. The Muslim Brotherhood, now gaining popularity in Egypt and Jordan and elsewhere in the Middle East, is one example of the approach. That of the Taliban (literally, "Students") in Afghanistan is another.

Conservative (other terms used include also *normative* and *orthodox)* fairly describes the style that likely characterizes the vast majority of Muslims. Cautious and suspicious of all major change, this approach prefers to let stand the full record of Muslim history. Because it tends toward political passivity, it has generally preferred even leadership judged deficient by Islamic religious norms, to revolution and anarchy. Saudi Arabia and Jordan might be fair examples.

The *adaptationist* (also called *acculturationist* or *modernist*) style favors fresh interpretation of Qur'an and Sunna in terms of changing needs. It takes a rather pragmatic view of politics, recommending leadership models on the basis of utility rather than Islamic legitimacy. Adaptationists encourage the incorporation of non-Islamic contributions to world culture, while at the same time raising Muslim consciousness about Islam's pioneering role in civilization. Twentieth-century Turkey might exemplify this style.

Finally, the *personalist* (or *charismatic*) style places the role of the inspired leader above all religious institutions, in fact if not in theory. Like the fundamentalist style, this approach also leans toward political activism and, if necessary, revolution, to bring about its version of a just Islamic society. Contemporary Iran represents a good example of the style, especially under Khomeini. In the history of Muslim religious institutions, one finds this approach represented particularly in Sufi religious orders. Those organizations originally developed around charismatic figures of legendary sanctity, called *shaykhs,* whose directives members accepted in blind obedience. The history of Christian religious orders offers numerous parallels.

89. What is the religious connection with the ongoing strife in Bosnia? What does all the talk about "ethnic" cleansing have to do with religion?

Islam began to develop a significant presence in the Balkans with the Ottoman conquest of 1463. Christianity had already been deeply rooted among the Catholic Croats and Orthodox Serbs for many centuries. Conversion to Islam, while generally not coerced by the Ottomans, was definitely associated with foreign domination. Although the Croats and Serbs have by no means always been peaceful neighbors, there have been periods of still greater hostility between the Christians, who have considered themselves the inheritors of the land, and the Muslims, whom they have often regarded as invaders. For many non-Muslim Bosnians, all things even remotely identifiable as Turkish represent the remnants of a historic scourge whose vestiges they would like to eliminate. Bosnian Serbs, with the urging of the government of Serbia in Belgrade, have been engaged in the systematic destruction of virtually every visible reminder of the Ottoman presence, which they associate with Islam. Scores of historic mosques, libraries, bridges, and other architectural treasures have been destroyed, all in an attempt to eradicate the identity of the Muslim people of Bosnia.

The peoples of the Balkans are generally of Western Slavic stock, so the term "ethnic cleansing" is an inaccurate description of recent events in the republics of the former Yugoslavia. Turmoil in the Balkans has resulted largely from political decisions that have sought to aggravate divisions among people of various religious communities who had been learning to live together peacefully. As such, the religious distinctions are decidedly secondary, but have proven to be handy tools for demagogues whose success depends on their ability to promote divisiveness and hatred.

90. Is there an "Islamic economics"?

Beginning with the Qur'an, Islamic tradition has had specific concerns about economic transactions in relation to economic justice. Muhammad himself had been a businessman, working with the caravan trade owned by his first wife, Khadija. As in so many other matters, Muslims find an exemplar in the Medinan society of the Prophet's day. One issue the Qur'an addresses at least indirectly is that of considering money as "product" rather than as a simple means of exchange. In effect the Qur'an regards money as a measure of goods and services, and not itself a basis for making more money.

Today, however, the world's banking and market systems are built on the concept that one can make money by loaning or investing it, without producing anything. So how do Muslims manage? Many, of course, have simply been going along with the "system." But there is increasing interest in devising creative ways to make money work according to the principle that all parties to financial transactions—not just the borrower—must share equally in the risk as well as the profits.

In other words, the focus of *all* parties is on the success of the project being funded rather than on the financial transaction. In addition, investors must screen their options carefully; the final criterion is not the promise of highest returns, but the certainty that the eventual product will be compatible with Islamic religious values (e.g., no stock in companies that produce weapons, alcohol, pornography, or in gaming concerns). In that same spirit, Islamic banking provides for interest-free loans to the truly needy.

Muslims engaged in implementing traditional Islamic values in today's global marketplace face a major challenge, but the goal is to ensure social equity and to keep the profit motive subordinate to a higher principle. This is Islam's major contribution to the evolution of business ethics in our time. Less adversarial than the financial arrangements most of us have become accustomed to, the emphasis in Islamic banking is on cooperation, so that the customer is primarily a partner.

Attempts to define "Islamic economics" as a discipline began in India during the 1930s and '40s, not long before the creation of Pakistan. In theory, Islamic economics stands somewhere between capitalist free enterprise and socialist control: it seeks to maintain market forces, but within the limits of broad social consciousness. But there is as yet nothing like consensus on a coherent theory among Muslim economists. The Qur'an, for example, forbids *riba,* a term generally understood to mean "taking interest," but economists do not agree precisely what that means for today. In practice, developments are largely limited to the field of banking. The first modern Islamic bank was established in Dubai in 1975, but over the past twenty years or so, the experiment has grown dramatically. Magazines geared toward Muslims now include increasingly numerous ads for businesses that invite participation from people looking for sound investment opportunities that are also religiously acceptable *(halal).*

91. What do Muslims think about environmental issues?

Beginning with the Qur'an, important Islamic texts and thinkers have addressed themselves to environmental issues. Take this text of the Qur'an for example: "Do they not see how each thing God has created, down to the very least, most humbly prostrates itself to God as its shadow revolves from the right and the left? To God all in heaven and on earth prostrates itself; from beasts to angels none withholds haughtily. In reverent fear of their transcendent Lord they do what they are bidden" (Qur'an 16:48–50).

Unlike the Bible, the Qur'an contains no integrated narrative of creation, suggests that God would surely need no rest after his "work," and hints that a "day" might actually be a very long time. In both sources Adam is the first human being, but the Qur'an's descriptions of the material out of which he was made vary from dust to semen to water to a clot of blood. Though the Qur'an's Adam also knows the names of all creatures, the emphasis is on God's knowledge rather than Adam's. In the Qur'anic stories, human beings are not created in God's image, for that would compromise the divine transcendence.

In general the Qur'an seems to place greater emphasis on God's sovereignty and power than does the biblical account. Whereas the Bible describes creation as a single original action, the Qur'an suggests that God is involved in creation as an ongoing activity, reasserting his creative prerogative with the emergence of each new living being. In the Bible, God seems to commission the first people unreservedly to take charge of the earth. Islamic tradition also regards the creation as given to humans to use, but God seems to hesitate a bit in turning the operation over to Adam and Eve. God offered to heaven, earth and the mountains the "trust" of watching over creation. They declined out of fear, so God offered the trust to humankind. Adam accepted, unjust and foolish as he was—and ungrateful in addition. When God informed the angels that creation would be entrusted to Adam as his representative (literally, caliph, vicegerent), they warned the Creator that human beings would surely act wickedly. God assured the angels that the risk was worth taking, for he had called forth from Adam's loins and assembled all of his yet unborn descendants and asked them, "Am I not your Lord?" They had responded as one and without hesitation, "Yes, we are witnesses to that!" (Qur'an 33:72; 2:30; 7:10, 172).

Any discussion of religious attitudes toward the care and keeping of our planet is bound to run head-on into the unpleasant fact that virtually no major religious community can boast a very impressive record in implementing its stated values. Unfortunately, greed quickly swamps lofty but fragile ideals in its wake. However unrealistic it may seem to speak of a tradition's ideals without taking a hard look at how human beings have actually behaved, ideals do need to be restated. My purpose here is neither to praise the Islamic community uncritically for its environmental concerns nor to condemn those Muslims who have played their part, along with the rest of us, in sacrificing the earth on the altar of the great god Profit.

92. News coverage of the Middle East in recent years gives the impression that there are many Muslims, with support from clerics, involved in terrorist activities. Is that an accurate impression?

Suppose you were a non-Christian living outside of the U.S.A., and the only thing you ever heard about Christians were reports of sectarian violence emanating from Northern Ireland. Would you conclude that Christians have a preference for violence? If IRA bombings and murders alone did not persuade you of that, suppose you heard credible reports that some Irish Catholic priests regularly gave their blessing to such activities. Suppose further that reports from that quarter were reinforced by occasional news of "Christian" bombings and assassinations at abortion clinics in the U.S.A. And suppose that you also heard accounts of how racist groups such as the Ku Klux Klan or the Aryan Nation regularly cloaked their social views in biblical and other religious teachings, and that organizations like them actively recruited with a message of hatred. Would that be enough to seal your opinion that Christianity and violence somehow go together?

Virtually everywhere people have appealed to religion to justify actions and policies that most persons of good will would condemn as incompatible with their religious beliefs. Just because people claim to belong to a particular religious tradition does not mean that they fairly represent that tradition. It merely means that unscrupulous people can sometimes twist and manipulate religion for evil purposes.

Part of the problem here is that there is sometimes a thin line between justifiable revolution and unlawful, treasonable action. How many colonial American preachers encouraged their congregations to support the "American revolution"? Whether in Northern Ireland or the Middle East, organizations like the IRA and Hamas have arisen to combat what they perceive as tyranny. Many of their members no doubt think of themselves as devout and sincerely religious. And many Irish-American Catholics and Arab-American Muslims who support these and other such causes financially no doubt regard their choices as highly ethical. But such support necessarily involves a terribly serious form of denial. It requires that one assert that no one on the "other side" is innocent, or at the very least, that one is sometimes forced to shed innocent blood to achieve a greater good.

Where does one draw the line? Both the Christian and Islamic traditions have sanctioned recourse to violent means to rectify blatant injustice. But mainstream teaching in both allows such action only in sheer desperation, only as a last resort, after pursuing *every* conceivable alternative. Nevertheless, both traditions encourage peaceful resolution to all conflicts. Islam, like Christianity, teaches in the strongest terms that terrorism is simply wrong. Nothing whatever in mainstream Islamic tradition and teaching defends any activity generally recognized as terrorism.

93. Jerusalem seems to be extremely important to the three Abrahamic traditions. Is that why the holy city remains such a bone of contention in Middle Eastern politics?

Each of the three Abrahamic faiths revolves around a sacred story, a distinctive interpretation of history. At the center of every sacred story is least one sacred place, which in turn carves out of the cosmos a space held to be inviolable and safe for believers—a sanctuary. For Jews, Jerusalem clearly focuses that sense of sacred place, and within Jerusalem it is the Western Wall (or Wailing Wall) that symbolizes Jewish identity above all. Here one can see and touch all that remains of the Solomonic and Herodian temples. Here one can lament the destruction of both temples and long for the raising of a new one. Unfortunately, time has made the situation agonizingly complex for Jews. The merest mention of rebuilding the temple evokes cries of outrage from the Muslim community, for on top of the temple mount there now stand the seventh-century shrine called the Dome of the Rock and the early eighth-century al-Aqsa mosque.

For Muslims the place recalls the importance of Abraham and

Solomon as prophets, and adds a new layer of sacrality in the belief that this place was a way station in Muhammad's chief mystical experience, the Night Journey and Ascension. The Muslim holy places on the temple mount also bear an important historic relationship to Christianity. Inscriptions on the Dome of the Rock, as well as the Dome's axial relationship to the al-Aqsa's basilical hall (which, it appears, was laid out to parallel and outdo that of the Sepulcher with its dome and basilical hall), clearly suggest a statement of Muslim superiority over Christianity. Muslims count as their own, in addition, the Mosque of the Ascension (of Jesus) on the Mount of Olives and the Mosque of Hebron that enshrines the cave of Machpelah, the tomb of Abraham and the patriarchs. Located as it is in an Arab town, the latter has been an important symbol for Palestinians.

For most Christians, the principal holy sites in the Middle East are of course the Church of the Nativity in Bethlehem, the Church of the Holy Sepulcher in Jerusalem, as well as several places in Nazareth. Perhaps no single place speaks more eloquently of the diversity of Christianity in the Middle East than the Holy Sepulcher. With its multiple side chapels representing various Christian communities, competing liturgical celebrations, and the olfactory dissonance that results from multiple flavors of incense, the Church of the Holy Sepulcher offers a virtual smorgasbord of the Christian tradition. It has been and remains an important symbol of Christian presence in Jerusalem. Christians have not always enjoyed free exercise of their rights in the Middle East, and access to the Sepulcher remains one symbolic anchor in their sense of identity. As a sacred city, Jerusalem is the single most important place in the Middle East. For Muslims, the Dome is a symbol of victory; for Jews, the Wall a symbol of loss; for Christians, the Sepulcher a symbol of victory through loss.

94. Could you sum up the history of the Israeli-Palestinian conflict? What role, if any, does Islam play in the current unrest in the Middle East?

Years ago a Palestinian friend told me this story: Once upon a time, a camel and a scorpion happened upon each other on the banks of a river. As the camel prepared to swim across, the scorpion approached and asked for a ride. When the camel refused for fear the scorpion would take advantage of his kindness and sting him to death, the scorpion explained how foolish that would be, for then they would both die. The camel agreed and began to ferry his passenger across. Halfway over the scorpion stung the camel. With his last gasp the dromedary asked, "Why on earth did you sentence us both to death?" Said the scorpion as the two went under, "Welcome to the Middle East!" You decide, my friend added, who is the camel and who the scorpion.

The conflict has deep historical roots but really began to assume its present proportions in 1917 when the Balfour Declaration established the British Mandate over Palestine and the Jewish population in the area saw a steady increase for thirty years. In 1947 the U.N. partition plan allocated 56 percent of the land, including prize seacoast, to the Jews, who constituted about a third of the population. The partition proceeded rapidly, and when Israel proclaimed statehood in 1948, the Arabs rebelled. Terror begot terror as the two sides confronted each other, but the Palestinians were steadily losing ground and being driven into exile as refugees. In 1956 the Suez crisis saw the last vestige of colonialism pitting America, Europe, and Israel against Egypt. Eleven years later Israel nearly doubled its territory in the Six Day War. In 1973 the Arabs fought back and managed to regain some ground. It was not until 1978 that the Camp David Accord began to turn events around, very slowly. But in 1982 Israel invaded Lebanon all the way to Beirut, laying siege until the PLO retreated. Israel has maintained its security zone in southern Lebanon since then. Then in 1987 the Palestinian uprising known as the Intifada resulted in massive Israeli curtailments of human rights and ongoing retaliation and counterretaliation by both Palestinian and Israeli interests.

Islam has been a powerful symbolic factor in contemporary Middle Eastern affairs, from the formation of alliances against Israel to the current rhetoric of Palestinian organizations like Hamas and Islamic Jihad. But this intractable conflict is not and never has been a "religious" war—many Palestinians are Christian, for one thing—but the use of religious imagery has become inevitable in a land where nearly every stone has sacred associations for someone.

95. What is an *Ayatollah?* And how much of Iran's foreign policy is actually religiously motivated?

The term *Ayatollah* is an honorific title conferred on a high-ranking religious scholar in the hierarchy of Twelver Shi'ism, the form of Islam dominant in both Iran and Iraq. A bit of history will help here. Three terms most commonly associated with Islamic religious officialdom everywhere are these: *ulama,* a general category that refers to all "learned" in religious matters; *faqih,* referring more specifically to those who exercise the formal function of *fiqh,* jurisprudence; and *mujtahid,* a title given to the most eminent of the *ulama* who have proven themselves fit to exercise *ijtihad,* independent investigation into and articulation of religious law. The Shi'i doctrine of the Greater Concealment of the Twelfth Imam (see Question 14) required the establishment of an authority structure capable of interpreting (fallibly) the mind of the absent (infallible) Imam. Hence, the exalted office of the *mujtahid.* Under the Safavid dynasty (1501–1722), mujtahids were few in number. Over the decades the religious institution witnessed a sort of honorific inflation, so that there are at present various ranks within the category of mujtahid, including two levels of *hujjatulislam,* "proof of Islam," and two grades of *ayatullah,* "sign of God," accorded by virtue of ability and size of constituency. Readers who have followed events in the Middle East over the past two decades or so have seen these terms often in the press.

Among top-ranking ayatollahs, several at any one time might be acknowledged as "sources of imitation" *(marja'-i taqlid).* Prior to the Iranian revolution, for example, Khomeini was reckoned as one of seven chief "sources of imitation." The period since the beginning of the Pahlavi dynasty (1925–79) has witnessed a dramatic "repoliticization" of Iranian Shi'ism. That came to a head when Ruhollah Khomeini returned to Iran to proclaim the end of the Pahlavi dynasty and the beginning of the Islamic Republic of Iran. Khomeini thus became the supreme lawgiver whose authority could not be questioned, for he represented the spiritual descendants of Muhammad, the Imams. His interpretation of Shi'i political theology marked a major departure from the classical doctrine, according to which the religious scholars generally functioned outside of political structures, often exercising the rights of a kind of loyal opposition. The end of the Iran-Iraq war and Khomeini's death in 1989 brought new challenges to the young revolutionary nation: questions of succession, the preservation of administrative structures in the absence of the charismatic leader, and accommodation to the world outside.

96. One often hears the term "Holy War" associated with certain groups who call themselves Muslims. Does the Qur'an teach this? Do most Muslims think it is a good thing?

Muslims and non-Muslims alike have unfortunately been using the term "Holy War" for a long, long time. The expression is an inappropriate rendering of the Arabic term *jihad,* whose root meaning is "striving" or "struggle." What Muslims mean when they use the term to describe external military and political activities is something like "religiously justifiable struggle against injustice and oppression." In other words, in its classical meaning the term *jihad* is roughly analogous to the Christian "just war theory." Most of the time the call for a *jihad* is 90 percent rhetoric, involving little or no serious reflection on what the tradition in its considerable depth and sophistication stipulates about criteria and conditions for waging a "just war." Political and economic considerations invariably intrude.

Many non-Muslims express misgivings about what appears to be the Islamic idea of "Holy War." They are often frankly afraid because they have formed the opinion that Islam is a violent religion. Many people have unfortunately and most unfairly come to expect that behind every episode of hostage taking or large-scale terrorism there lurks a band of swarthy, bloodthirsty Arab or Iranian Muslims. Every time journalists use the term *jihad,* either as part of some faction's name or to describe the "holy war" some Muslim leader has allegedly called for, millions of listeners or readers have their worst fears confirmed. "There they go again!" one hears people say too often, citing such examples as Khomeini's death sentence on Salman Rushdie and Saddam Husayn's attempts during the Gulf War to galvanize Islamic support for a Jihad against all infidels defiling sacred Arabian soil.

97. What are the criteria or guidelines Muslims use for deciding when a *jihad* is appropriate?

Questions abound concerning the sanctioning of violent means, which Islamic tradition shares with more than one other major religious tradition. There is no doubt that it is an important issue about which we need to understand several complex aspects.

First, Muhammad stands out as the ideal model for fostering peaceful relations among groups of people in conflict. When envoys from Yathrib (later Medina) came south to Mecca offering Muhammad and his followers a new home, part of what they wanted in return was that Muhammad arbitrate the tribal disputes then troubling their city. Tradition emphasizes Muhammad's preference for peace and the centrality he accorded to the reconciliation of hearts. Still it is exceedingly difficult to see through the veil of dark images that has shrouded the non-Muslim image of Muhammad over the centuries. When non-Muslims read, for example, of Muhammad's decision to fight the Jewish tribes of Medina, they are shocked. Unfortunate events like these seem to blind us to anything positive in the early history of Islam. At the opposite end of the spectrum, Muhammad remains for Muslims the paragon of gentleness and concern for the needs of people.

Second, the vast majority of Muslims long for a world at peace. They sincerely believe that Islamic values seek to promote the possibility of such a world. Their tradition, they believe, stands not only for the absence of war, but for that positive state of safety, security, and freedom from anxiety that uniquely results from a grateful surrender to God in faith *(islam, iman)*. We must also remember that Muslims have children, too. They have no desire to see their sons or daughters, brothers or sisters go off to war to be killed or maimed. Everyone's blood runs red. And when it does, we all suffer.

Third, Islamic criteria governing the call for a jihad against an outward enemy are as stringent as Christianity's terms for waging a "just war." Moreover, Muslim specialists differ as widely as do Christian theologians as to the circumstances under which one can claim to have met those criteria. In addition, one must distinguish between popular sentiment and the core of a faith tradition. Most Muslims are as unfamiliar with the classic conditions for jihad as their Christian counterparts are with their tradition's criteria for a "just war." According to

Muslim tradition, for example, no action can be justified as authentic jihad if any of the following conditions obtain: killing noncombatants, prisoners of war, or diplomatic personnel; use of poisonous weapons (beginning with poison-tipped arrows and swords, for example), or inhumane means to kill; atrocities in conquered lands, including mutilation of persons and animals, and wanton despoliation of natural resources; and the sexual abuse of captive women. All of that, however, has not prevented horrors from being perpetrated in the very name of Islam, to the great sorrow of many millions of Muslims. Nothing can excuse those who engage in such atrocities, whatever their express motivation, whatever their avowed religious affiliation.

Finally, the issue of colonialism is one that most westerners rarely think about, but which is of great concern to many in the Middle East, North Africa, and South Asia, especially to the Muslims living in these regions. It was once said that "the sun never sets on the British Empire." This was so because Britain had colonized vast portions of the globe from the British West Indies in our own backyard all the way to India and beyond. Throughout the Middle East and North Africa many of the territories occupied by both the British and the French were primarily Muslim, former lands of the rapidly declining Ottoman Empire. Regrettably, the native populations of these regions were rarely treated well. Many Palestinians, for example, are convinced that the current unrest in their region exists because the British, French, and even the United Nations cheated them out of land that had been theirs for centuries. Many Muslims still feel that actions taken by the United States—American involvement the Persian Gulf war is but one example—represent nothing more than the old colonialism in new clothes. Colonialism is a sore issue with Muslims all over the world. As we try to understand the motivations behind alleged Islamic calls for "Holy War," all of these issues must be kept in mind.

98. Could you describe the growth of Islam in the U.S.?

Islam took root here much the same way Judaism and Christianity did, a nonnative tradition imported with the expansion of Western Europe. What differs though is that the first Muslims in the New World did not come voluntarily; they came as slaves. Many early slaves came from West Africa, and perhaps as many as 20 percent of African slaves brought during the eighteenth and nineteenth centuries were Muslim. Because they were slaves, these early Muslims had little chance to nurture the spread of their faith in any formal ways. That process would begin only in the late nineteenth century with an influx of mostly Arab Muslims from the Middle East. The period between the two world wars saw a second major migration; a third commenced just after World War II and continued for some twenty years. Unlike earlier immigrants, who had sought wealth that they could take back home later, those who came in subsequent waves were often fleeing political oppression. With requirements for entry to the United States stiffened in the mid-1960s, the most recent phase of immigration has included well-educated Muslims from a variety of countries, and notably from South Asia (India, Pakistan, Bangladesh).

A second aspect of Islam's growth in America is its presence among African Americans. The story is one of fascinating sectarian developments, especially over the past fifty years or so. Most readers will have heard of the "Black Muslims," and many non-Muslim Americans still think the term refers to those African Americans once associated with Elijah Muhammad. Actually, apart from members of prison populations, among whom there are many converts to Islam, most Black Muslims in America are now members of mainstream Muslim communities. The stories of these African American Muslims offer great insight into how they adapted to their new way of life, as minorities both by race and by faith.

One last small contingent of American Muslims is made up of indigenous, mostly female, white converts. Some become Muslim so as to share the faith of a spouse, but many women say that they find Islam attractive because they believe it accords women greater dignity than American society in general. A still smaller number of Americans consider themselves at least incidentally Muslim by virtue of their belonging to "Sufi" groups that trace their spiritual lineages to the mystical organizations mentioned in question 49. I use the term *incidentally* because such groups often place greater emphasis on human unity than on membership in an Islamic faith community.

99. How would you say the growing Muslim presence is being received here?

Unfortunately, the growing presence of Islam in this country frightens many Americans. They have come to associate the very mention of Islam with strangeness and mystery and, alas, violence. The challenge now facing many American non-Muslims is that of understanding our Muslim neighbors as fellow citizens and brothers and sisters in the human race. The facts of religious and social change invite us all to stretch our notions of who and what "belongs" in our land. Americans generally have been very good at rising to that challenge.

From six to eight million Muslims now live in this country. The Islamic centers in Washington, D.C., and Perrysburg, Ohio, are but two of the more physically impressive institutions of their kind that have appeared on the American landscape over the past several decades. Such centers of Muslim identity now number well over a thousand. Most are quite simple and ordinary in appearance, for they are merely converted residences, buildings that once housed small businesses, or even former Christian churches and schools. More and more, these places are becoming a concrete indication of the growth of Islam as an American religious tradition. At their present rate of growth, Muslims will in twenty-five years constitute the second largest faith community in the U.S. Whatever the actual count, it is clear that Islam is no longer "over there somewhere."

People often ask, "What goes on in those Islamic centers?" The answer in general is simple: very much the same kinds of things that go on in churches and synagogues. Their primary function is that of mosque (Arabic *masjid,* literally "place of prostration"), though most manage to make room for a wide range of activities. As mosques they need first of all to provide for their members' ritual needs, including especially a place to perform the ablution before *salat.* But both because the development of secondary institutions needs time and financial resources, and because Islam has always adapted to its surroundings, American Muslim centers are used for everything from child care and religious education to youth activities and potluck dinners, to public lectures and fund-raising appeals. Some of the older and better-established centers include specific facilities for the broader range of activities. Perrysburg, for example, has a large room adjacent to the prayer hall for meetings and presentations, as well as a full kitchen and eating facility on the lower level for social gatherings. Plans call for a large expansion, including a separate educational wing and residential facility. Together these places of prayer and social gathering represent the collective aspirations of Muslims in America to establish a community of faith and values in which family and social solidarity can flourish.

100. What is the "Nation of Islam"? And who are the "Black Muslims"?

Formal identification by African Americans with things at least nominally Islamic dates back to early this century, with Noble Drew Ali's founding of the Moorish-American Science Temple. Remnants of the movement that began in Newark can still be found here and there, its male members including the Turkish term for a nobleman, *Bey,* as part of their religious names.

A much more important development began in Detroit during the 1930s. There a little-known character named W. D. Fard offered African Americans a way of identifying with their African roots: their ancestors had been Muslims and it was time to rediscover their heritage. When Elijah (Poole) Muhammad joined the group, "The Lost-Found Nation of Islam in the Wilderness of North America," Fard bestowed upon him the mantle of prophetic office. Elijah's message had little in common with basic Islamic teachings and amounted to a form of reverse racism. Still, the Nation of Islam, the group's shortened title, offered the benefits of an enhanced sense of self-dignity and many positive community-building values.

One of the Nation's most famous members was Malcolm (Little) X. The most formative influence on Malcolm X was his pilgrimage to Mecca. There he found that, contrary to Elijah's message of racial segregation and black superiority over white, everyone "snored in the same language." Malcolm returned full of a conviction of human equality, eventually disavowed Elijah Muhammad's teachings, and was assassinated in 1965. Malcolm's dissent deeply influenced Elijah's son Wallace, and when in 1975 the elder Muhammad died, Wallace began the process of sweeping reforms with the intention of bringing the community into line doctrinally with mainstream Islam. That involved a frank repudiation of Elijah's most cherished views. Taking the religious name Warith Deen (close to the Arabic for "heir to the religion"), he led the community through a series of changes of name and identity over the next eight years. Its name was changed to the American Bilalian Community, and its newspaper called *Bilalian News* (Muslim tradition records that Muhammad chose as his *muezzin* an Abyssinian named Bilal, the first black convert to Islam). Today those whose roots go back to Elijah Muhammad have divided into two main groups. The majority followers of Warith Deen have come more and more to be integrated into the larger American Muslim community, while followers of Louis Farrakhan still identify themselves as the Nation of Islam and carry on the separatist spirit of Elijah Muhammad. The majority of African American Muslims no longer consider themselves a distinct religious society and have dropped such former names as World Community of Islam in the West and American Muslim Mission.

✻✻✻✻✻✻✻✻✻

101. You've devoted so much time and effort to learning about Islam. Have you ever considered becoming a Muslim? How has your study affected your own faith?

Muslims especially have often asked me that, issuing me a cordial invitation along with it. Through my twenty-five years of studying Islam as a religious tradition, however, I have never been moved to consider converting. That is not because I do not find it an attractive tradition, but because I regard my faith and my membership in the worldwide community of Roman Catholics as a gift to be cherished and nurtured. Nor on the other hand have I ever suggested to any of my students that they might consider becoming Muslim, or to any of my Muslim friends and acquaintances that they would be better off as Christians. Nevertheless, the study of Islam is much more than a dry academic exercise for me. Islam is, for me, one of God's signs. Islam is a challenge, a risk, a source of encouragement, and a call to take a bigger view of what life on this planet is about.

Jesus challenged the people of his time not to be complacent about being the "chosen" people, challenged them to read the signs of the times. The question for me is, how large am I prepared to allow God to be? How inclusive is God's love? If my religious affiliation comes between me and God's other children, it may very well come between me and God too. Risk often goes hand in hand with challenge. Jesus says to the Samaritan woman in the Gospel of John: "The hour is coming when neither on this mountain nor in Jerusalem will you worship the Father....The hour is coming, and it is now, when the true worshipers will worship the Father in spirit and truth, for such the Father seeks to worship Him" (Jn 4:21, 23). I believe the study of Islam has been part of my call, not to a diminished personal commitment to my faith, but to the risk of living in the uncharted territory "between" Gerizim and Jerusalem.

My experience as a student of Islam has been one of hope, encouragement, and often of profound spiritual consolation. I have found the beauty of the scripture and the literary and visual expression of the tradition's religious values deeply moving and uplifting. The increasingly evident fact of religious pluralism in our world convinces me daily of the need to seek a more adequate understanding of what motivates Muslims as well as members of other faith communities. Instead of being discouraged that the vast majority of people are not Christian and are not likely to become Christian, I am encouraged that so vast a multitude who call themselves Muslims seek God with a sincere heart.

Finally, the very fact of Islam calls me to a conversion more radical than any transfer of confessional allegiance. It is a call to expanded awareness. Islam is part of my world, a world about which Vatican II calls for a new vision: "Over the centuries many quarrels and dissensions have arisen between Christians and Muslims. The sacred Council now pleads with all to forget the past and urges that a sincere effort be made to achieve mutual understanding; for the benefit of all,...let them together preserve and promote peace, liberty, social justice and moral values." Isaiah calls to mind God's global vision as well: "I will say to the north, Give them up; and to the south, Do not hold back. Bring my sons from afar and my daughters from the ends of the earth, everyone who is named as mine, whom I created for my glory, whom I formed and made" (Is 43: 6–7).

APPENDIX: INVENTORY OF ATTITUDES TOWARD ISLAM

An interesting exercise for classes, study groups, or individuals learning about Islam for the first time might be to take the following questionnaire informally before reading the material. Then take it again afterward, to see how your views and attitudes have changed. Use the answer blank on the left as your "before" response and on the right as your "after" response. Discuss the outcome with others in your class or study group.

I. Availability of Information about Islam and Muslims:

Answer each item by choosing one of the possible answers to the following statement. "During the past two or three years I have...": 1) Often 2) Seldom 3) Can't recall 4) Very rarely 5) Never

_____ read something that made me feel positive   _____
toward Islam.
_____ read something that made me feel negative   _____
toward Islam.
_____ seen in the media something that made me feel   _____
positive toward Islam.
_____ seen in the media something that made me feel   _____
negative toward Islam and Muslims.
_____ had a positive conversation with a friend about   _____
Islam.
_____ had a negative conversation with a friend about   _____
Islam.

_____ talked seriously with a Muslim about religious   _____
matters.

_____ talked casually with a Muslim about anything at   _____
all.

_____ read a helpful book about Islam.   _____

_____ heard a non-Muslim religious person give a talk   _____
that was positive toward Islam.

_____ heard a non-Muslim religious person give a talk   _____
that was negative toward Islam.

_____ observed a Muslim prayer service or other reli-   _____
gious observance.

_____ met a Muslim in a professional or social setting.   _____

II. To evaluate the *kind* of information that has been available to you up till now, answer the following by choosing the appropriate number:

_____ Allah is: 1) the Arabic word for God 2) the god   _____
Muslims alone worship 3) another name for
Muhammad.

_____ Muhammad came from what is now: 1) Syria 2)   _____
Saudi Arabia 3) Iran.

_____ Islam began about: 1) 3000 2) 600 3) 1400 years   _____
ago.

_____ The Qur'an is: 1) a country in the Middle East 2)   _____
Islam's sacred book 3) a Muslim dietary code.

_____ There are presently about: 1) 200,000 2) 25 mil-   _____
lion 3) 6–8 million Muslims living in the U.S.A.

_____ Islamic law permits Muslim men to marry: 1) four   _____
wives 2) one wife 3) as many as they want.

_____ Muslims believe Muhammad was a: 1) prophet 2)   _____
god 3) politician and merchant.

_____ Muslims are encouraged to pray 1) once 2) 3 times   _____
3) 5 a times day.

_____ When Muslims pray they always turn toward: 1)   _____
Mecca 2) Medina 3) Jerusalem 4) Tehran.

_____ Ramadan is: 1) a festival 2) a month of fasting   _____
from sun-down to sunrise 3) a Sufi group.

_____ The two major groups of Muslims are called: 1)   _____
Sunni and Hanafi 2) Shi'i and Sunni 3) Sufi and
Sunni.

_____ A man who sought to change the style of Islam of   _____
Elijah Muhammad was: 1) Louis Farrakhan 2)
Muhammad Ali 3) Malcolm X.

_____ There are about: 1) 200 million 2) 400 million 3)   _____
one billion Muslims worldwide.

_____ Muslims worship in: 1) temples 2) mosques 3)   _____
minarets 4) synagogues.

_____ Muslims believe Islam: 1) is equal to Christianity   _____
and Judaism 2) completes the revelation given
to Christians and Jews 3) is equal to Judaism
but inferior to Christianity.

_____ The country with the largest Muslim population in   _____
the world is: 1) Saudi Arabia 2) Iran 3) Indone-
sia 4) Egypt.

**III. To give a better idea as to your awareness of and attitudes
toward Islam and Muslims, answer the following questions with:
1) Yes/True 2) No/False 3) Not Sure.**

_____ It is important for American non-Muslims to   _____
understand Islam.

_____ Islam is a valid religious approach to life and   _____
deserves a hearing.

_____ Muslims worship Muhammad as a deity.   _____

_____ Jesus and Moses are both important figures for   _____
Muslims.

_____ Muslim beliefs were mostly borrowed from   _____
Judaism and Christianity.

_____ Most Muslims are more religious than are Jews   _____
and Christians.

_____ Muslims are almost all foreigners.   _____

_____ Most Muslims are Arabs.   _____

_____ Islam is probably a dangerous force in today's world.   _____

_____ Muslims are always eager to engage in a Holy War.   _____

_____ Muslims believe that to die in a Holy War insures heavenly reward.   _____

_____ Though there are Muslim "fanatics," other religions also have their "fanatics."   _____

_____ Muslims tend to be more warlike than members of other religions.   _____

_____ Islam probably spread by means other than the sword.   _____

_____ The way Muslims mix religion and politics scares me.   _____

_____ Muslims seem to value life less than Jews and Christians.   _____

_____ Muslims are just ordinary human beings, like the rest of us.   _____

_____ Islam does not condone terrorism any more than does Christianity.   _____

_____ People like Saddam Hussein and Khomeini give Muslims a bad name.   _____

_____ The future of world peace is directly linked to the ability of various religious groups to understand and tolerate their differences.   _____

_____ There are probably no Muslims living in my city.   _____

_____ Muslims ought to be given consideration where they work if they wish to take time off to pray during the day.

_____ Muslims should be allowed to leave work on Friday to go to a mosque.   _____

_____ Muslims who fast because of their religion should get special consideration at work.   _____

_____ Employers and places of business should be considerate of Muslims' dietary sensitivities in providing food services.   _____

_____ There should be only one set of laws for all Americans, and no one should be allowed to appeal to religious law as a way around civil law. _____

_____ My family would be angry if I married a Muslim. _____

_____ My family would be angry if I married outside my religion. _____

_____ As long as members of other religions don't force their views on me, they can do as they please within the laws of the land. _____

_____ I firmly believe in "freedom of religion." _____

_____ Muslims who want to set up Islamic schools to educate their children ought to be allowed to do so. _____

_____ I would not be bothered if Muslims moved into my neighborhood. _____

_____ I would be very upset if the quiet of my neighborhood were interrupted by a Muslim call to prayer five times a day. _____

_____ The United States is a Christian country and members of other religions will just have to get used to that. _____

_____ I am interested enough in finding out about Islam that I would be willing to go to a Muslim prayer service. _____

_____ I know of the location of a mosque in my city. _____

_____ I have attended a Muslim prayer service. _____

_____ It seems to me that Islam is a valid and acceptable approach to life. _____

_____ I feel I know all I need or want to know about Islam and Muslims. _____

_____ All members of religions other than my own are going to hell. _____

_____ If I were invited to join a religious dialogue group involving members of my religious tradition and Muslims, I would consider joining it. _____

_____   I have met people who suggested to me that I   _____
          ought to become a Muslim.
_____   I have thought of becoming a Muslim.   _____
_____   When I watch or listen to international news I am _____
          struck by the prominence of Islam and Muslims
          in world affairs.
_____   Not enough is being done to safeguard the rights _____
          of Arab Americans to Free Speech.
_____   News media reporting of Middle Eastern events   _____
          seems generally fair and balanced.
_____   The Palestinians are really only interested in the _____
          destruction of the state of Israel.
_____   News coverage of the situation of the Palestinian _____
          Arabs strikes me as being skimpy and often
          biased against them.

SUGGESTIONS FOR FURTHER READING

Barboza, Steven, et al. *American Jihad: Islam After Malcolm X*. New York: Doubleday, 1994.

Blair, Sheila S., and Jonathan M. Bloom. *Islamic Art*. London: Phaidon, 1997.

Denny, Frederick M. *An Introduction to Islam*. 2nd ed. New York: Macmillan, 1994.

Esposito, John L., and John O. Voll. *Islam and Democracy*. New York: Oxford University Press, 1996.

Goddard, Hugh. *Christians and Muslims: From Double Standards to Mutual Understanding*. Surrey: Curzon Press, 1995.

Haddad, Yvonne Y., and Adair T. Lummis. *Islamic Values in the United States*. New York: Oxford University Press, 1987.

————, ed. *The Muslims of America*. New York: Oxford University Press, 1991.

Hodgson, Marshall. *The Venture of Islam: Conscience and History in a World Civilization*. 3 Vols. Chicago: University of Chicago Press, 1974.

Lapidus, Ira M. *A History of Islamic Societies*. Cambridge: Cambridge University Press, 1988.

Lee, Martha F. *The Nation of Islam: An American Millenarian Movement*. Syracuse: Syracuse University Press, 1996.

Malti-Douglas, Fedwa. *Woman's Body, Woman's Word: Gender and Discourse in Arabo-Islamic Writing*. Princeton: Princeton University Press, 1991.

Martin, Richard. *Islamic Studies: A History of Religions Approach*. 2nd ed. New York: Prentice-Hall, 1996.

Mernissi, Fatima. *Beyond the Veil: Male-Female Dynamics in a Modern Muslim Society*. Cambridge, MA: Schenkman, 1975.

Murata, Sachiko, and William C. Chittick. *The Vision of Islam*. New York: Paragon House, 1994.

Phipps, William E. *Muhammad and Jesus: A Comparison of the Prophets and Their Teachings*. New York: Continuum, 1996.

Renard, John. *Seven Doors to Islam: Spirituality and the Religious Life of Muslims*. Berkeley: University of California Press, 1996.

Renard, John, ed. *Windows on the House of Islam: Muslim Sources of Spirituality and Religious Life*. Berkeley: University of California Press, 1998.

Rippin, Andrew. *Muslims, Their Religious Beliefs and Practices: The Formative Years*. New York: Routledge, 1990.

————. *Muslims, Their Religious Beliefs and Practices: The Contemporary Period*. New York: Routledge, 1993.

Robinson, Neal. *Christ in Islam and Christianity*. Albany: State University of New York Press, 1991.

Schimmel, Annemarie. *Deciphering the Signs of God: A Phenomenological Approach to Islam*. Albany: State University of New York Press, 1994.

Sells, Michael A., ed. and trans. *Early Islamic Mysticism*. New York: Paulist Press, 1996.

INDEX

(This index contains selected persons, places, events and themes to help you find your way through the text. Numbers following entries indicate the *question* in which that entry is found.)

in Qur'an: 69; and polygyny: 83; and jihad: 96; converts to Islam: 98; *see also* divorce, family
works: 28; of mercy: 74
worship: 38, 42, 47, 51, 57, 64, 70; in Gospel of John: 101

Yathrib: *see* Medina
Yemen: 63

Zahra: 44
zakat: see almsgiving
ziyara: see pilgrimage
Zoroastrianism: 2, 10, 12, 64

Other Books in the Series

RESPONSES TO 101 QUESTIONS ON THE BIBLE
by Raymond E. Brown, S.S.

RESPONSES TO 101 QUESTIONS ON THE DEAD SEA SCROLLS
by Joseph A. Fitzmyer, S.J.

RESPONSES TO 101 QUESTIONS ABOUT JESUS
by Michael L. Cook, S.J.

RESPONSES TO 101 QUESTIONS ABOUT FEMINISM
by Denise Lardner Carmody

RESPONSES TO 101 QUESTIONS ON THE PSALMS AND
OTHER WRITINGS
by Roland E. Murphy, O. Carm.

RESPONSES TO 101 QUESTIONS ON THE CHURCH
by Richard P. McBrien

RESPONSES TO 101 QUESTIONS ON THE BIBLICAL TORAH
by Roland E. Murphy, O. Carm.

RESPONSES TO 101 QUESTIONS ON BUSINESS ETHICS
by George Devine

RESPONSES TO 101 QUESTIONS ON DEATH AND
ETERNAL LIFE
by Peter C. Phan